Disaster Preparedness Planning for the Homeless:

Practices & Gaps

Disaster Preparedness Planning for the Homeless:
Practices & Gaps

R.R. Erickson, Ph.D.

Grizzly Walk Publishing Group, LLC

www.grizzlywalkbooks.com

Disaster Preparedness Planning for the Homeless: Practices & Gaps

Copyright © 2018 E.R. Sebastian

All rights reserved.

ISBN-13: 978-1976106903

Cover Image (#226036692) is the work of @Marcus and is licensed through Adobe 2019.

Printed in the U.S.A.

Grizzly Walk Publishing Group, LLC

Missoula, MT 59802

www.grizzlywalkbooks.com

Acknowledgements

I would like to thank all the people at Northcentral University who reviewed my work, provided feedback, and offered me encouragement over the duration of my doctoral project. I would also like to thank my family, who kept me motivated and focused on completing what I started. Without the support of these individuals, I would not have finished this dissertation or brought light to a serious disaster preparedness deficit.

Table of Contents

ABSTRACT xiv

CHAPTER ONE: INTRODUCTION 1

    Statement of the Problem.. 9

    Purpose of the Study 11

    Conceptual Framework... 12

    Nature of the Study 14

    Research Questions... 19

    Significance of the Study.. 20

    Definitions of Key Terms.. 21

    Summary 24

CHAPTER TWO: LITERATURE REVIEW...................................... 27

    Theoretical/Conceptual Framework for Studying Disaster Preparedness.. 36

    Emergency and Disaster Management Cycle 53

    All-Hazards Approach to Emergency and Disaster Management 64

    Holistic Planning... 68

    Studies on Disaster Preparedness 70

    Summary 87

CHAPTER THREE: METHODOLOGY 89

    Research Methodology and Design 90

    Population and Sample 101

    Materials and Instruments... 104

Study Procedures 106

Data Collection and Analysis 109

Assumptions 111

Limitations 112

Delimitations 113

Ethical Assurances 113

Summary 114

CHAPTER FOUR: FINDINGS 117

Trustworthiness of the Data 118

Results 121

    Alabama 147

    Alaska 149

    Arizona 151

    California 153

    Colorado 156

    Connecticut 158

    Florida 160

    Illinois 162

    Indiana 164

Minnesota 166

Montana.. 168

New Mexico... 170

New York 172

Oregon.. 174

Texas 176

Washington.. 178

Washington, D.C.. 180

Wisconsin 182

  Evaluation of the Findings 183
  Summary 191
CHAPTER FIVE: IMPLICATIONS,
RECOMMENDATIONS, & CONCLUSIONS................... 194
  Implications 196
  Recommendations for Practice 202
  Recommendations for Future Research 208
  Conclusions... 209
REFERENCES 212

Appendix A: Best Practices 240

Appendix B: Current Practices 240

Appendix C: Checklist of Best Practices 241

Appendix D: Analysis Level B 241

Appendix E: BIA Questionnaire 242

Appendix F: Standardized Disaster Preparedness Plan
Outline for Organizations Serving the Homeless 243

ABSTRACT

The problem addressed by this study was the American failure to meet the disaster preparedness needs of the homeless. The purpose of the study was to assess the gaps between the best practices for disaster preparedness, as identified by FEMA and emergency and disaster management experts, and the current disaster preparedness activities completed by all organizations that offer disaster services to the homeless. The study included content analyses, a gap analysis, spatial data analyses, and the triangulation between the case studies found in the literature review and the study's findings. The research questions asked were, "What are the best practices recommended by experts in managing the special needs of the homeless in regard to the emergency and disaster management processes: Mitigation, Preparedness, Response, and Recovery," "What disaster preparedness steps are addressed by homeless shelters and other disaster service providers for the homeless," "What gaps exist between best practices recommended by FEMA and other experts and what homeless shelters and other disaster service providers for the homeless are currently doing regarding emergency and disaster preparedness planning," and "What vulnerabilities are created by the gaps in disaster preparedness planning for the homeless in the United States?" The findings showed a great deal of variability in best and actual practices when planning for the disaster needs of the homeless, that disaster preparedness was ineffective, and that the homeless were suffering unnecessarily because of the deficits. The conclusions drawn were that disaster preparedness mandates were needed for homeless shelters and service providers to standardize disaster preparedness processes. Future research is required in order to explore the implementation of disaster preparedness plans and their outcomes.

CHAPTER ONE: INTRODUCTION

The defining characteristic for emergency and disaster management in the 21st century was the deepened interest in disaster preparedness. The Department of Homeland Security (DHS) defined emergency and disaster preparedness as "a continuous cycle of planning, organizing, training, equipping, exercising, evaluating, and taking corrective action in an effort to ensure effective coordination during incident response" (DHS, 2017, para. 1). By this definition, an incident was an emergency or disaster that required the mobilization of significant amounts of community resources (DHS, 2017). The severity and scope of damage produced by disasters, which included the terror attacks on Washington, D.C., New York, New York, and Shanksville, Pennsylvania on September 11, 2001; Tropical Storm Allison of 2001; Hurricanes Charley, Francis, Ivan, and Katrina in 2005; the Evansville Tornado in 2005; and Hurricane Rita in 2005; escalated interest in disaster preparedness (Burby, 2006; Eshghi & Larson, 2008; Okal et al., 2005; Schuster et al., 2001). Each of these disasters had a price tag of well over $500 million, demonstrating the rising financial threat posed by large-scale incidents (Smith, 2007). To reduce the threat of multi-million or billion-dollar crises in the future, disaster preparedness systems are designed to minimize risks, losses, and costs of disasters.

The damage produced by the disasters from the first decade of the 21st century was significant, but both the immediate and long-term recovery efforts could have been significantly improved, with resulting financial benefits, had the right preparedness strategies been in place (Gamboa-Maldonado, Marshak, Sinclair, Montgomery, & Dyjack, 2012; Miceli, Sotgiu, & Settanni, 2008). FEMA (2017) recommends that localities and states utilize an all-hazards approach to disaster preparedness. The all-hazards approach creates a single disaster preparedness plan to cover all hazards (Paton, 2013). Since this approach creates a general response plan for the average citizen in the jurisdiction, holistic planning strategies need to be added to ensure the special needs of sub-groups found within the community are identified and addressed (Gamboa-Maldonado et al., 2012). The holistic approach to emergency and disaster preparedness required as many stakeholder groups as possible to participate in emergency and disaster planning activities, including representatives for the homeless population (Gamboa-Maldonado et al., 2012).

To be effective, holistic planning is best done on the local level, because local populations and service providers are experts in the risks, needs, and capabilities of the community (Sylves, 2014). Subsequently, the local level is where FEMA assigns the majority of emergency and disaster preparedness responsibilities and authority, as this is where first responders are positioned and where resources are easiest to access (Sylves, 2014). The hierarchy of disaster response is local, state, and then federal governments (Sylves, 2014). However, while local emergency and disaster management departments accept the responsibility of being the primary agent of emergency and disaster preparedness, resource limitations restrict the scope of locality mitigation, preparedness, response, and recovery to general preparedness for the community as a homogenous whole (Chandra et al., 2013).

The restriction of the scope of local government preparedness impairs the efficacy of the holistic approach to disaster preparedness. Specifically, it limits the ability of local emergency and disaster management departments to effectively identify and address the preparedness issues associated with vulnerable populations, such as the homeless (FEMA, 2017). The main problem keeping local EDMs from planning for special populations is that EDMs routinely fail to recruit or include representation from vulnerable populations found within the community in preparedness activities (Reininger et al., 2013). A vulnerable population is defined as a population that has an impaired ability to function in society and to respond effectively to emergency and disaster situations because of social, economic, physical, psychological, or emotional limitations (Chong et al., 2014).

The lack of representation of homeless populations or their advocates is dangerous because homeless populations accounted for 549,928 people across the United States in 2015, and populations have continued to grow slowly since (U.S. Department of Housing and Urban Development, 2016). To understand the special needs of this subpopulation fully, some form of representation is needed on disaster preparedness planning committees for the homeless. Representation can be members of the homeless population, advocates for the homeless, service providers to the homeless, or a combination of people from these groups. The representation will provide important planning information, insights, and resources that are currently missing from the government disaster preparedness process (Walters & Gaillard, 2014). By filling this gap of representation and knowledge, the heightened state of risk experienced by the homeless during emergencies and disasters can be mitigated (Walters & Gaillard, 2014).

While FEMA recognizes this oversight, it places the responsibility for disaster preparedness planning for special needs populations, including the homeless, onto organizations that serve the population or the people with special needs themselves (Walters & Gaillard, 2014). This is problematic for a number of reasons, including the fact that the homeless and organizations that serve the homeless have limited resources for preparedness and do not have access to the expertise needed to effectively establish disaster preparedness plans (Gin, Kranke, Saia, & Dobalian, 2015). Subsequently, homeless people cannot prepare for disasters and service providers for the homeless must piece together preparedness plans, if they indeed create them, using what information is available online and using their own judgement (Every, 2016). These practices create incomplete and inconsistent disaster preparedness, limiting the ability of the homeless to access resources and help during an emergency or disaster. When the process is assessed, the problem is a gap in roles and responsibilities associated with disaster preparedness for the homeless. First, city emergency and disaster management departments do not understand the needs of the homeless, and successively expect that homeless advocacy groups and shelters will address these needs. Second, homeless advocacy groups and shelters do not have disaster preparedness knowledge, skills, and abilities, so they expect that the city's emergency and disaster management department will take care of disaster preparedness efforts. In the end, no one is planning or preparing to meet the disaster preparedness, response, and recovery needs of the homeless.

The current standards for emergency and disaster preparedness began as a response to the aftermath of the events of September 11, 2001, and the passing of the Homeland Security Act of 2002 (Public Law 107-296, 2002). The objective of Homeland Security Act was to centralize all federal resources used to protect homeland interests and security under one agency figurehead, the Department of Homeland Security (Public Law 107-296, 2002). By centralizing homeland security functions and agencies, interagency collaborations and information sharing were made more efficient. One of the benefits of centralizing national security functions and agencies, in terms of emergency and disaster management for the United States, was that the centralization of homeland security efforts encouraged the adoption of a standardized approach for emergency and disaster preparedness (Public Law 107-296, 2002, Title I; Waugh & Streib, 2006). The standardized process for emergency and disaster preparedness was the all-hazards approach introduced by the Federal Emergency Management Agency (FEMA) (Paton, 2013; Von Lubitz, Beakley, & Patricelli, 2008). This approach created one general preparedness plan for all hazards a community faced (Paton & Johnston, 2017). While this was an efficient method of preparedness planning, it failed to help communities effectively plan for the special needs of vulnerable populations (Walters & Gaillard, 2014). For example, it did not identify how to locate the homeless, who did not have physical addresses, it did not establish what specialty services were needed for mental and physical health needs of special populations, and it failed to account for the need to provide transportation for the homeless who did not have transportation of their own to use for evacuations or to move to shelters.

One of the first tests of the all-hazards approach to emergency and disaster preparedness planning, following the passing of the Homeland Security Act, was Hurricane Katrina (Walters & Gaillard, 2014). Hurricane Katrina was not only devastating because of the damage caused by the hurricane, storm surges, and failure of the levee, but also because it demonstrated how ill-prepared communities were to deal with the special evacuation, sheltering, and recovery needs of vulnerable populations (Laditka et al., 2008). Horror stories emerged as news crews moved into New Orleans to report on the impact of the disaster. However, while stories of nursing home residents being abandoned by their caretakers, people sheltering in sports arenas, escalated violence and crime at disaster shelters, and the massive loss of property in New Orleans attracted the attention of the media and researchers, no one talked about the homeless or the reality that the homeless were viewed as a disposable part of the population by the local, state, and federal governments responding to the crisis (Moynihan, 2012). For example, a study by Moynihan (2012) reported that the most underserved population during the Hurricane Katrina response was the homeless. Part of the problem was that public policies were not in place to authorize the procurement of resources, such as boats, to support rescue efforts for the homeless (Moynihan, 2012). Additionally, since the homeless did not have a formal address, search and rescue teams did not have a list to use to identify individual homeless in the impacted areas who needed help. Consequently, the homeless were left in dire situations with little hope of being looked for, rescued, or provided with assistance (Moynihan, 2012).

The lack of concern over the homeless in emergency and disaster situations in the first part of the 21st century created a humanitarian crisis (Moynihan, 2012). The homeless were just as human as property owners and renters, and they had a right to emergency and disaster response and recovery services just like any other resident in a community (Gin et al., 2016). However, the lack of representation of homeless or organizations that serve the homeless on disaster preparedness planning committees produced gaps in preparedness for the homeless. This was seen in the failure to authorize efforts and resources to rescue the homeless during the Hurricane Katrina disaster, as well as in the lack of concern about moving the homeless to shelters and helping them to recover from the disaster (Moynihan, 2012). These examples demonstrated that the all-hazards approach to preparedness has deficits in terms of understanding and meeting the special needs of vulnerable populations (Fogel, 2017; Moynihan, 2012). Furthermore, these examples suggested that for communities to meet the special disaster preparedness needs of homeless populations, communities need to create effective preparedness plans that address the specific needs and vulnerabilities of the homeless.

Statement of the Problem

This study addressed the problem of a failure to plan adequately for the special disaster response and recovery needs of the homeless, a vulnerable population, resulting in devastating consequences (Coe, Moczygamba, Harpe, & Gatewood, 2015). According to Moynihan (2012) it took weeks to authorize boats to evacuate the homeless stranded in the flooded city of New Orleans following Hurricane Katrina (Moynihan, 2012). The effects of inadequate planning for the homeless during disaster preparedness activities were also highlighted in Fogel's 2017 study that collected data from focus groups of homeless who had survived natural disasters in California, New York, or Florida. Fogel reported that the homeless were denied assistance post-disaster because they did not have identification, a physical address, or a phone number, and the disaster management agencies failed to communicate with the homeless about where to access shelters and resources (Fogel, 2017). Fogel reveals that local governments and private organizations serving homeless populations during disasters are both failing to understand the disaster preparedness and response needs of the homeless. Consequently, the homeless are denied assistance and/or only offered help as a matter of chance when the homeless person happens to cross paths with first responders or other aid providers. Finally, the organizations that do offer services to the homeless are severely limited in their support capabilities because of small operational budgets and limited access to disaster preparedness expertise (Every, 2016). As a result, the reach and efficacy of the help offered to the homeless are grossly limited. This is a service gap, and social injustice, that needs to be corrected. By correcting this, when disasters occur, the homeless will be offered equitable disaster response and recovery services as the rest of the population.

Purpose of the Study

The purpose of the study was to assess the gaps between the best practices for disaster preparedness, as identified by FEMA and emergency and disaster management experts, and the current disaster preparedness activities completed by all organizations that offer disaster services to the homeless. The results identified what aspects of disaster preparedness for the homeless need to be improved. This purpose was conceptualized by first establishing what emergency and disaster preparedness activities were being done for the homeless by homeless shelters and other organizations, and then determining if there were gaps in the preparedness activities observed when compared to the best practices for emergency and disaster preparedness, contingency planning, and disaster resiliency development currently being used at the community level of emergency management.

A contextual analysis was conducted with a structuralist approach, which was a qualitative methodology commonly used by researchers conducting policy studies (Bemelmans-Videc, Rist, & Vedung, 2011). The data utilized in this study came from the emergency and disaster preparedness manuals and policy documents developed by organizations that manage homeless populations in communities in the United States. This included homeless shelters, homeless advocacy groups, social services organizations, and local offices of emergency and disaster management. It was critical to identify gaps in preparedness efforts for homeless populations to make it possible to evaluate if best practices created by experts in disaster preparedness are effectively being implemented for the homeless, and if not, to identify gaps in the implementation of best practices to determine what changes are needed to promote equality of distribution of disaster preparedness services to the homeless (U.S. Department of Health and Human Services, 2013).

Conceptual Framework

The conceptual framework guiding the current study is comprised of two components, disaster resiliency and contingency planning. Disaster resiliency is the ability to experience a crisis and recover to pre-crisis status quickly with few long-term consequences or deficits (Paton & Johnston, 2017). Resiliency is created through preparedness, training, and ongoing social support (Fletcher et al., 2016). This aspect of the framework is important because it helps to reduce risks of long-term psychological problems developing as a result of the crisis, such as Post Traumatic-Incident Stress Disorder (Fridman, Alkozei, Simth, Challener, & Killgore, 2017). In application to the problem of emergency and disaster preparedness for homeless populations, it is critically important to develop resiliency within the population and the organizations that serve the homeless, because homeless populations are already disadvantaged in regard to resource access, especially mental and physical health care (Coe et al., 2015).

The second element of the theoretical framework is contingency planning. Contingency planning is simply having one or more alternatives if the first option for responding to a crisis is disabled, no longer safe to use, or becomes overwhelmed with demand for its use (Boin, Stern, & Sundelius, 2016; Booth, 2015). Contingency planning involves identifying key functions and creating redundancy within the system, such as having backup communication options, alternative sites for sheltering during the crisis, and having multiple evacuation routes planned out (Stambler & Barbera, 2015). Contingency planning is important when preparing organizations that serve the homeless for a crisis situation, because the population of people needing assistance can increase rapidly, overwhelming the existing facilities, and since homeless do not have transportation or shelter of their own, both of these resources need to be provided (Fogel, 2017; Rahm & Reddick, 2011).

Both the resiliency and contingency elements of disaster preparedness for homeless populations are integrated together in an all-hazards emergency and disaster preparedness and response plan. This plan follows FEMA guidelines, and includes sections on mitigation, which will address resiliency development; preparedness, which will address contingency planning; response, which will address the immediate threats posed by the disaster; and recovery, which outlines how the organization will return to pre-disaster status (Paton & Johnston, 2017). While described linearly, the steps are cyclic, meaning that once recovery is nearing completion, the mitigation stage starts again (Paton & Johnston, 2017). Using this model, the content of existing preparedness plans for the homeless can be assessed for completeness.

Nature of the Study

The nature of the study was a content analysis. The content analysis utilized a structuralist approach to evaluate themes in content found in the various planning and preparedness documents used by organizations serving homeless populations, such as homeless shelters. It also evaluated themes found in the federal model for disaster preparedness created by FEMA (2017). The design of the content analysis used best practices for the methodology, including the implementation of strategies for promoting the reliability of conclusions derived from the documents sampled (Elo et al., 2014). Strategies used include effective coding practices, the application of qualitative-based data analysis techniques, and appropriate sampling techniques for qualitative studies (Elo & Kyngas, 2008).

The content analysis was selected for the current study because of two primary reasons. The first reason was that little was known about how communities prepare for the disaster response needs of the homeless (Fogel, 2017). Therefore, a qualitative study design was appropriate, as the situation needed to be described in detail. The second reason why a content analysis was selected for the current study was that preparedness for emergencies and disasters was communicated via documents, namely an emergency and disaster preparedness and response plan (Paton & Johnston, 2017). Since the preparedness practices were documented in formal plans, it made sense to sample data from those plans to learn more about trends in disaster preparedness for the homeless.

The content analysis section of the study involved two levels of data analysis. In the first level of analysis, Level A, general findings about current practices in preparedness for the homeless were established. Level A analysis began by identifying best practices, as defined or established by experts in the field of emergency and disaster preparedness, such as FEMA and textbooks on emergency and disaster management. A sample of eight expert sources was collected and analyzed. This sample was sufficient because best practices for disaster preparedness should be consistent on the major points of planning, and only deviate slightly based on the organizational or professional area of expertise. For example, business experts provided more disaster preparedness steps directed at protecting business operability, whereas humanitarian organizations, such as the Red Cross, provided best practices for securing the health and well-being of people during a disaster. Descriptive statistics, such as frequency and percentages were used to identify what preparedness activities were considered to be best practices. The study defined a best practice as being present in disaster preparedness planning by a sampled expert. For current practices, strategies were listed according to their prevalence in the documents surveyed and prioritized from most prevalent to least prevalent.

Step two of the data analysis created a checklist of best practices and determine if current practices at the organization level were meeting each best practice listed. To be considered as meeting a best practice, the best practice needed to be present in at least 75% of the current practice documents sampled from organizations serving the homeless during disasters. The answers were tallied and averaged. Current practices were considered insufficient if the score was below .75 and considered acceptable if the score is at or above .75.

Step three assessed what improvements were needed to fill in current practices gaps for disaster preparedness for the homeless. This step involved listing each missing best practice, so that appropriate mitigation strategies could be developed. When appropriate, a process to cover groups of missing best practices was presented instead of providing individual recommendations for each missing best practice.

The second level of analysis, Level B, described to what extent each best practice was executed in the sampled current practices documents. Level B analysis began by creating a list of the best practices that were identified as being used by the documents sampled in Level A. Each best practice was analyzed by sample to calculate a grade of completion of the best practices. To establish the grade of completion, the coding used a scale of one to ten. A score of one equated to superficially addressed. This meant that the best practice was only minimally developed. For example, if the best practice was to develop a contingency plan and the homeless shelter only created a list of alternative shelter sites without including an evacuation plan that explains how to move residents/clients to the alternative shelter, then this item will be scored as superficially addressed. A score of five equated to the average engagement of the best practice. This meant that the best practice item was developed according to expert recommendations, including supporting plans and documentation. Finally, a score of ten equated to being fully developed, meaning that not only were the recommended items/tasks completed, but additional development above the recommendations were also present. The scores for each best practice were tallied and averaged to determine what best practices need the most work, and to determine the overall level of effort organizations serving the homeless are putting into their disaster preparedness.

The next part of the study was a spatial data analysis. This part of the study involved the creation of GIS maps for the states sampled in Dataset A, the best practices data, and Dataset B, the current practices data. The GIS maps showed where disasters were declared between 2012 and 2017, as well as where homeless shelters were located within the state. A spatial analysis was conducted in which overlaps in homeless shelter locations and disaster declarations occurred. The vulnerability level of homeless shelters during a disaster was assessed by frequency of how many homeless shelters were impacted by a disaster declaration between 2012 and 2017.

The final part of the study was a triangulation analysis. This analysis involved correlating the data from the gap analysis, spatial data analysis, and literature review. Triangulation was used to identify potential implications of the findings from the current study and to abstract meaning from those findings.

Research Questions

To guide this study, it was important to evaluate what experts in managing the special needs of the homeless recommended for each phase of the emergency and disaster management cycle. The four phases were mitigation, preparedness, response, and recovery (Reddick, 2011). The following research question is posed:

RQ1: What are the best practices recommended by experts in managing the special needs of the homeless in regard to the emergency and disaster management processes: Mitigation, Preparedness, Response, and Recovery?

In addition to knowing the best practices for emergency and disaster preparedness planning, it was also necessary to identify what organizations in charge of care for the homeless are actually doing. To identify strengths and weaknesses of the current preparedness efforts, the following research question must be answered:

RQ2: What disaster preparedness steps are addressed by homeless shelters and other disaster service providers for the homeless?

Next, to understand the level of preparedness that exist, the following research question was asked:

RQ3: What gaps exist between best practices recommended by FEMA and other experts and what homeless shelters and other disaster service providers for the homeless are currently doing regarding emergency and disaster preparedness planning?

Finally, to clarify the focus and main objective of the study, the last research question was posed:

RQ4: What vulnerabilities are created by the gaps in disaster preparedness planning for the homeless in the United States?

Significance of the Study

Since the first decade of the 21st century, FEMA recommended that organizations utilize an all-hazards approach to emergency and disaster planning (Paton & Johnston, 2017, p. 2185). This approach simplified disaster preparedness, but it created deficits in the ability of organizations to address the needs of populations with special needs, such as the homeless (Every, 2016; Fogel, 2017). When all-hazard emergency and disaster plans have addendums that are supposed to address special needs populations, these sections are often superficially constructed without any input from the population they are intended to serve (Fogel, 2017). This puts the majority of the responsibility for planning and preparing for the emergency and disaster response effort for the homeless population in a community on organizations that serve the population, such as homeless shelters (Walters & Gaillard, 2014). The current study of preparedness strategies for homeless populations will produce findings that homeless shelters, homeless advocacy agencies, state and local emergency management departments, and policymakers, will view as valuable, as it will establish the level of disaster preparedness among homeless shelters operated by American churches. This information will be most valuable to researchers, policymakers, government agencies, and homeless organizations in communities with large homeless populations, such as Los Angeles, Miami, Washington, D.C., and New York City, but it will also provide good guidance for smaller communities as well. The wide scope of value is created by the structure of the disaster preparedness documents being reviewed. They are a framework of best practices and major steps to take, so they are applicable to all organizations serving the homeless, regardless of their locality or climatic concerns.

Definitions of Key Terms

Best practice. Taylor, Godin, Garnholz, Lin, and Cohen (2017) defines this term as a process or procedure proven through empirical evidence and/or historical precedent to produce the desired results consistently.

Critical incident. An emergency, disaster, or crisis that is severe enough to overwhelm the norming coping and response mechanisms of the person, organization, or communities, and requires a strategic response to control short- and long-term consequences effectively (Paton & Johnston, 2017).

Emergency and disaster preparedness. The DHS (2017) defines emergency/disaster preparedness as "a continuous cycle of planning, organizing, training, equipping, exercising, evaluating, and taking corrective action in an effort to ensure effective coordination during incident response" (para. 1). This term can also be called disaster preparedness, emergency preparedness, or just preparedness. These terms are used interchangeably.

Emergency and disaster management process. The complete process an organization, government, or individual uses to manage disaster situations. The process includes the following steps: mitigation, preparedness, response, and recovery (Haddow, Bullock, & Coppola, 2013).

Homeless. A condition in which a person does not have a permanent place of residency because of inadequate access to the resources needed to secure housing (Amore, Baker, & Howden-Chapman, 2011).

Homeless shelter. For the purposes of this study, a homeless shelter is an institution that offers lodging and other services to the homeless as a part of its normal business activities (Rojas-Guyler, Inniss-Richter, Lee, Bernard, & King, 2014).

Local emergency management department. Most cities and towns have a local emergency management department. This is the agency that is responsible for managing local disasters and emergencies. It orchestrates disaster preparedness, planning, responses, and recovery efforts (Haddow et al., 2013).

Mitigation. Efforts exerted to reduce risks and to build up resilience to a disaster (Haddow et al., 2013).

Planning. Conscious effort to evaluate risks/hazards and develop a plan of action to respond to them before they cause an incident (Haddow et al., 2013).

Preparedness. Planning ahead to manage the challenges of a disaster situation, including creating a disaster response plan, stockpiling resources, identifying evacuation routes, and coordinating efforts with other people and organizations to respond effectively to an emergency or disaster situation (Haddow et al., 2013).

Recovery. The process or restoring the organization to its pre-disaster state (Haddow et al., 2013).

Resilience. The ability to recover to pre-disaster conditions as quickly as possible after a disaster strikes (Haddow et al., 2013).

Response. The actions taken when a disaster occurs to secure an organization and its members, and to protect assets and human life from hazards posed by the disaster and its immediate aftermath (Haddow et al., 2013).

Vulnerable population. A vulnerable population is defined as a population that has an impaired ability to function in society and to respond effectively to emergency and disaster situations because of social, economic, physical, psychological, or emotional limitations (Chong et al., 2014).

Summary

The United States invested a considerable amount of time and money developing an efficient and effective emergency and disaster management system (FEMA, 2017). However, despite gallant and successful efforts to plan for general populations, the homeless population was neglected in terms of planning for their disaster preparedness, response, and recovery needs (Fogel, 2017). Subsequently, serious consequences of this oversight devastate homeless populations when disasters strike.

As a result of the neglect and to correct for this oversight, the current study sampled emergency and disaster preparedness plans from organizations that offer disaster services to the homeless. To answer the research questions posed, a four-part study design was implemented. The four parts were a content analysis, gap analysis, spatial data analysis, and triangulation analysis. The content analysis examined themes relating to what preparedness strategies were used by the organizations sampled. The results of the analysis identified trends in disaster preparedness strategies used by organizations serving the homeless during disasters, as well as identified gaps between what was done and what emergency and disaster experts recommend as best practices for disaster preparedness. The spatial data analysis assessed the impact that disasters from 2012 to 2017 had on homeless shelters in the states sampled. The impact was quantified as a frequency. Finally, the triangulation analysis compared findings from the content analysis, gap analysis, and spatial data analysis to the findings summarized in the literature review. Comparisons were used to identify potential implications of the findings from the current study. The information was published in a report and made available to researchers, organizations serving homeless populations, and to other government, non-profit, and private agencies interested in disaster preparedness. By incorporating the information in this report and including homeless representation in the planning process, government agencies and homeless advocacy groups will be better able to serve the unique needs of the homeless before, during, and after disasters.

CHAPTER TWO: LITERATURE REVIEW

The United States is known for being the land of opportunity, meaning that everyone has an equal chance at the American Dream of being successful and having a home, family, and high standard of living (McQuiggan, 2016). However, few people actually achieve the American Dream because of the huge disparities in how the nation's wealth and resources are distributed. Subsequently, about 0.17% of the population experiences homelessness each day (U.S. Department of Housing and Urban Development, 2016). While this may seem insignificant, it accounts for more than a half million men, women, and children who are disadvantaged, without shelter, and vulnerable to threats posed by normal and disaster-related factors (U.S. Census Bureau, 2016).

United States' homeless population profile. In the United States, an estimated 549,928 people experience homelessness on any given day (U.S. Department of Housing and Urban Development, 2016). This population is diverse in its makeup. To understand the diversity better, it is helpful to examine the population of the homeless in the U.S. by age, household type, and subpopulation. When considering age, 22% are under 18 years of age, 9% are between the ages of 18 and 24, and 69% are over the age of 24 (U.S. Department of Housing and Urban Development, 2016). However, when considering household type, the demographic distribution of age groups changes. For example, the population of people living as individuals and who are also homeless has the following age distribution: 1% of the population of individuals are under 18, 10% are between 18 and 24, and 89% are older 24 (U.S. Department of Housing and Urban Development, 2016). Family groups experiencing homelessness have the following age distribution: 60% are under the age of 18, 8% are between 18 and 24 years of age, and 35% are over the age of 24 (U.S. Department of Housing and Urban Development, 2016). Finally, when evaluating the distribution of homelessness among subpopulations in the United States, the primary group that is homeless is veterans. This subpopulation makes up 97% of all homeless populations, with and without children (U.S. Department of Housing and Urban Development, 2016). While the number of veterans who are homeless is chronic and severe, equally as concerning is the number of unaccompanied children and young adults at homeless shelters. In January 2016, 3,925 children under 18 were unaccompanied at homeless shelters in the United States, and 31,761 young adults between 18 and 24 were counted as unaccompanied at American homeless shelters (U.S. Department of Housing and Urban Development, 2016).

The distribution of age and subpopulations among the homeless in the United States indicates a significant demand for sheltering options. The ability for the homeless to access sufficient sheltering options, however, varies greatly by the demographic traits of the individuals. When the entire homeless population is evaluated for sheltering status, for example, 29% of the population is made up of individuals who go unsheltered, 36% of the population is made up of individuals who are sheltered, 32% of the population are families who are sheltered, and 3% are families who are unsheltered (U.S. Department of Housing and Urban Development, 2016). These statistics demonstrate that nearly 40% of all homeless in the U.S. do not have access to emergency, temporary, or other sheltering options.

The data on the demographic distribution of homeless in the United States is presented in Table 1. The data shows that most homeless are male, non-Hispanic, and white. These trends hold true for "All Homeless People," "Sheltered People," and "Unsheltered People" (U.S. Department of Housing and Urban Development, 2016). While this is interesting information, not much value can be derived from it because most of the U.S. population is also male, non-Hispanic, and white. Since this is the only information provided by the U.S. Department of Housing and Urban Development (2016) from their survey, no further inferences can be made.

Table 1 - Homeless Distribution in the United States 2016

Characteristic	All Homeless People		Sheltered People		Unsheltered People	
	Count	%	Count	%	Count	%
Total	549,928	100	373571	100	176357	100
Gender						
Female	217,268	39.5	165,780	44.4	51,488	29.2
Male	330,890	60.2	206,999	55.4	123,891	70.3
Transgender	1,770	0.3	792	0.2	978	0.6
Ethnicity						
Non-Hispanic	428,629	77.9	286,430	76.7	142,199	80.6
Hispanic	121,299	22.1	87,141	23.3	34,158	19.4
Race						
White	265,660	48.3	163,881	43.9	101,779	57.7
African American	215,177	39.1	168,623	45.1	46,554	26.4
Asian	5,603	1	3,476	0.9	2,127	1.2
Native American	15,229	28	7,880	2.1	7,349	4.2
Pacific Islander	8,734	1.6	4,499	1.2	4,235	2.4
Multiple Races	39,525	7.2	25,212	6.8	14,313	8.1

While the issue of homelessness in the United States is significant, the data indicates the situation is improving, although slowly. For example, homelessness among individuals declined less than 1% between 2015 and 2016. However, homeless family counts seem to be improving, showing a decline of 6% in the families counted at shelters in 2015 when compared to families counted at shelters in 2016 (U.S. Department of Housing and Urban Development, 2016). It is unclear what this decline actually means. For example, the U.S. Department of Housing and Urban Development (2016) does not know why the count is declining because data is not collected on why people do not use a homeless shelter.

Geographic distribution of homeless. While every state in the United States has a homeless population, a standard rate across all states does not exist. The five states with the highest rates of homelessness are California (22%), New York (16%), Florida (6%), Texas (4%) and Washington (4%) (U.S. Department of Housing and Urban Development, 2016). The states with the highest unsheltered homeless rates (rate of homeless who are not in shelters) are California (66.4%), Oregon (60.5%), Hawaii (54.4%), Nevada (53.1%), and Mississippi (48.9%). In contrast, the states with the lowest unsheltered homeless rates are Rhode Island (3.2%), Nebraska (3.7%), the District of Columbia (3.8%), Massachusetts (3.9%), and New York (4.2%) (U.S. Department of Housing and Urban

Development, 2016). These contrasts are important to note because (1) the states with the lowest unsheltered homeless rates are the states where homeless shelters and services are most developed, and (2) the states with the lowest unsheltered homeless rates are also the states where too many nights without shelter can lead to death. Subsequently, these are the states that are ideal to study in terms of their disaster preparedness for the homeless.

Responsibility for managing the homeless. In the United States, responsibility for disaster management takes a bottom-up position. The bottom-up position means that responsibility in an emergency or disaster situation starts with the individual and progresses upward through society to local groups, local government, regional governments, state governments, and finally the federal government (Haddow et al., 2013). This hierarchy is intended to reduce the utilization of government resources until it is necessary. The bottom-up position encourages each person or family to take steps to prepare to manage their personal needs for up to 72 hours following a disaster (Haddow et al., 2013). This lag time is needed to stabilize and secure the community so that first responders can reach community members and begin to distribute aid. While the 72-hour preparedness level is reasonable to ask of the average citizen in a community, it is not a reasonable request of people who are homeless, as they do not have the ability to stockpile food and water for a disaster situation (Every & Thompson, 2014; Settembrino, 2017). Since the homeless are largely dependent on homeless shelters and other social services offered by local agencies, it is the agencies that serve the homeless that currently are being tasked with the responsibility to prepare for the special needs of the homeless during a disaster response (Gin et al., 2015). This includes sourcing additional housing options for the homeless during disasters, planning for an influx of homeless into shelters during and after disasters and providing medical care to the homeless who were exposed to the hazard or its secondary impacts (Haddow et al., 2013; Walters & Gaillard, 2014).

The problem with assigning all of the disaster management responsibilities to the service providers for the homeless population is that the service providers are not being included in the community and state level holistic planning teams (Gin et al., 2015). As a result, local and state level planning teams do not know the size of the homeless population or its special needs, which impairs the planning team's ability to prepare for the special needs of the homeless, and service providers to the homeless are unaware of what resources are available to help meet the sheltering and care needs of the homeless before, during, and after a disaster strikes (Every & Thompson, 2014, p. 52; Settembrino, 2017). The impact of this disconnection between the government level planning team and the service providers charged with helping the homeless to survive a disaster is that resources are available that are not being used, and the homeless are denied the resources that they need to survive disaster situations. These are inefficacies that need to be addressed.

Roadmap. In Chapter Two, a critical review of the literature is presented. It provides an in-depth discussion of the theoretical/conceptual framework selected for the research project, an exploration of related constructs and practices for disaster preparedness, and an exploration of studies conducted on disaster resilience in general and for homeless shelters. The literature review involves an in-depth survey of available studies and authoritative references using the following keyword search phrases: disaster preparedness, disaster resilience, contingency planning, disaster recovery plans, homeless shelter disaster preparedness, agreements for alternative sites for the homeless during disasters, disaster recovery contingency planning, FEMA and contingency plans, recovery plan and opportunity for improvements, services offered by homeless shelter, critical functions of homeless shelter, disaster resilience and recovery plans, organization disaster resilience and mitigation, preparedness and psychological resilience, preparedness and disaster resilience, and building disaster resilience. This discussion is followed by a review of studies on disaster planning for the homeless using the identified strategies.

Theoretical/Conceptual Framework for Studying Disaster Preparedness

Since the events of September 11, 2001, the United States has perceived disasters as an inevitability, as opposed to a possibility. The new tableau adopted is that Americans need to be prepared, "Not if, but when" disasters strike (Gandy, Kern, Norton, & Toth, 2014, p. 1). While the foundation of the new American emergency and disaster management construct was built on the emergency and disaster management cycle, all hazards disaster planning, and holistic planning paradigms, when studying disaster preparedness at the organizational level, disaster resilience and contingency planning reveal more meaningful information about disaster preparedness.

Disaster resilience. Disaster resilience means that a person, organization, or community has the ability to recover quickly from a critical incident to pre-disaster status (Paton & Johnston, 2017). Resilience has many advantages that organizations benefit from including less severe disruptions to business, shorter periods of reduced functionality, and less stress on employees, customers, and other stakeholders (Cavallo & Ireland, 2014; Cutter, 2013). To build disaster resilience, simple steps needs to be followed.

Building resilience. One task associated with building resilience is to engage in mitigation for known risks (Cavallo & Ireland, 2014). Mitigation efforts do two things. First, they create resistance to disaster impacts (Cavallo & Ireland, 2014). For homeless shelters, mitigation efforts to create resistance to damage would include creating safe rooms that will protect employees and clientele from flying debris and other hazards posed by high speed winds associated with tornados and hurricanes. Second, mitigation efforts can minimize the damage created by the disaster (Cavallo & Ireland, 2014). In this scenario, the efforts will provide an extra layer of protection from the threats posed by identified hazards. For example, a homeless shelter could install air filters to protect residence, employees, and volunteers during active threats posed by smoke, toxic fumes, and other noxious and/or toxic air born pollutants.

Another step to take is for managers of the organization to engage in preparedness activities (Cutter, 2013). Studies show that the simple act of preparedness builds psychological resilience to the stressors and trauma of disasters (Aldunce, Beilin, Handmer, & Howden, 2014; Brassett & Vaughan-Williams, 2015; Plough et al., 2013). The reason for this is that the act of preparing for a disaster makes people feel as if they are in control of the situation. When the people feel in control of the situation they experience less stress when a disaster strikes, not only reducing the risks for long-term psychological complications caused by the disaster, but also helps to prevent short-term cognitive impairments from disaster-related stress (Brassett & Vaughan-Williams, 2015). Subsequently, an organization that has employees and clientele that are *prepared* for a disaster respond more effectively to the chaos and stress of a disaster. To harvest this benefit, managers need to involve stakeholders in the preparedness process (Aldunce et al., 2014). For example, managers can create a preparedness planning team that includes employees from different departments, customers, and vendors. This strategy is known as holistic planning and it enhances the efficacy of the disaster preparedness created (Haddow et al., 2013).

 Preparedness and resilience is supported by establishing an understanding of what resilience is and what is required to consider an organization resilient to disasters. Cutter, Burton, and Emrich (2010) recommend using benchmarking baselines for disaster preparedness. These benchmarks are created by evaluating best practices recommended by experts in disaster preparedness, as well as recommendations made by professional organizations that shape disciplinary practices (Cutter et al., 2013). Once the best practices for disaster resilience are established, Arbon (2014) further recommends the development and implementation of metrics of disaster resilience for the organization. This involves identifying best practices and establishing how well that practice should be developed. For example, a best practice for disaster resilience is to engage in preparedness activities, and the level of development that is needed for minimum disaster resilience is to meet the basic recommendations made by FEMA for organization preparedness (Cutter et al., 2013). To complete a manager's understanding of organization-level disaster resilience, he/she needs to analyze the organization's resilience strategies to identify strengths and weaknesses, as well as to evaluate how effective the practices have been in the past (Zobel & Khansa, 2011).

Another step to take to build disaster resilience is to develop a business continuity plan. A business continuity plan identifies critical functions for the business and then creates strategies for maintaining these functions during and immediately after a disaster (Sahebjamnia, Torabi, & Mansouri, 2015). For a homeless shelter, the critical functions are to provide food, shelter, clothing, personal hygiene supplies and showers, and in some cases, protection from abuse (Fuehrlein et al., 2014). To ensure these services can continue to be delivered during a disaster, homeless shelters need to develop contingency plans, which will be discussed in detail in the next section, for supplies and for shelter. Usually, this will involve working with other organizations to locate buildings large enough to handle overflow or to relocate the homeless if the shelter is damaged or at risk for damage during a disaster (Fuehrlein et al., 2014).

The final step is to create an effective recovery plan. Effective recovery plans detail what steps the organization needs to take to respond to a disaster situation, to stabilize the physical assets of the organization, to get employees back to work, and to continue the delivery of services to customers (Sahebjamnia et al., 2015). The recovery plan also includes a list of resources that can be tapped to help the organization to recover. For example, homeless shelters can contact social services organizations; local, state, and federal government agencies for grant money; and private citizens and organizations in the community for help in rebuilding and restoring the homeless shelter to its pre-disaster (or better) condition. Ideally, the recovery plan will help the organization to take advantage of opportunities to improve its disaster resilience, to build stronger infrastructure, and to building stronger relationships with stakeholders (Berke, Smith. & Lyles, 2012; Sahebjamnia et al., 2015).

Strengths and weaknesses. The decision to invest in building resilience needs to be backed by strategic business advantages to justify the cost. One such advantage is the creation of co-benefits. A co-benefit is when the organization gains more than just resilience to disaster through their resilience building efforts (Mechler, Mochizucki, & Hochrainer, 2016). For example, if the company becomes self-sufficient in generating its own energy to combat the risks posed by lost utilities during a disaster, then this company would both develop disaster resilience and reduce its energy costs. To get the most value from co-benefits, organizations need to approach resilience building strategically (Mechler et al., 2016).

Another advantage offered by building disaster resilience is that it makes employees and leaders within the organization mindful of what factors impact the company's functionality and performance (Fekete, Hufschmidt, & Kruse, 2014). This is an important advantage, because it encourages employees to scan their daily work environment for risks or warnings of impending threats that will have a negative impact on the organization. Once identified, leaders and employees can work together to develop strategies for responding to these threats before they cause damage (Fekete et al., 2014).

The process of resilience building also offers benefits that enhance daily and disaster response performance. The first benefit is that it helps to enhance organizational cohesion by providing opportunities for employees and managers to work together to solve problems (Eisenmann et al., 2014). The more opportunities employees have to work together with managers to promote the sustainability of the organization, the more invested employees become in promoting the success of the organization. The reason for this is that by including employees in decision making and problem-solving processes, employees feel that their success/failure is directly tied to the company's success/failure (Crawford, Rich, Buckman, & Bergeron, 2014). Subsequently, resilience building activities improve organizational resilience to disaster, engage employees, promote group cohesion, and inspire employee loyalty to the organization.

When done properly, resilience building is well worth the investment of time, money, and effort. However, the process can be a waste of company resources if it is not done properly (Sommer, Howell, & Hadley, 2016). The first error that managers can make when building resilience is not defining what they mean by the term *resilience* (Lowe, Sampson, Grueber, & Galea, 2015). Resilience has many different connotations, so it is essential that a manager create an operational definition of the term that fits the needs and expectations of the organization. This definition will serve as a metric of success, as well as a focusing factor for the resilience building team. Failure to effectively define resilience can lead to inefficacies in building resilience, misunderstandings about what employees should be doing to make the organization more resilient, and costs can become unmanageable as different people attempt to create competing models of disaster resilience for the organization (Lowe et al., 2015; Sommer et al., 2016).

Another mistake that homeless shelter managers can make while attempting to build disaster resilience is to follow the disaster resilience plan developed for another homeless shelter or company verbatim (Sommer et al., 2016). While a manager may assume that a disaster resilience plan is universal in its design, or at least universal among similar sized companies in the same industry and market, this is not the case. While the structure may be universal regardless of the organization using the resilience plan, the details of the plan need to be customized for the specific characteristics of the organization, its location, its employees, and its operation (Sommer et al., 2016). Subsequently, each company needs a unique resilience plan for the plan to be effective. Failure to create a unique plan for a company increases the chances that managers will spend time and money building resilience strategies that are irrelevant or unnecessary for the organization, as well as likely missing needed resilience capabilities (Bristow & Healy, 2014). Either of these oversights puts the organization at risk for being negatively impacted by a disaster, up to and including the failure of the company and the loss of life.

Contingency planning. FEMA stated that at the very least, all organizations should invest in creating contingency plans for their critical functions (Sittig, Gonzalez, & Singh, 2014). Contingency planning involves creating redundancy in the supply chain and communications. Redundancy in supply chains is achieved by identifying and creating plans to access resources during disaster response and recovery to supplement the normal resources used by the organization (Sittig et al., 2014). For homeless shelters, this will include identifying alternative sites where the homeless can be channeled if the normal homeless shelter building is too small to accommodate the expanded demand for sheltering the homeless during a disaster, and/or the normal homeless shelter is or is expected to be damaged by the disaster. To secure these alternative sites and supplies, the manager of the homeless shelter needs to establish formal agreements with other organizations, including the local government, so that when a disaster strikes, the alternative sites can be set up quickly to accommodate the influx of homeless (Soltani, Ardalan, Boloorani, Haghdoost,

& Hosseinzadeh-Attar, 2015). The homeless shelter manager also needs to work with the local department of emergency and disaster management, so that they are informed about where the temporary shelters will be located and if transportation will be provided.

To create redundancy for supplies, the homeless shelter manager needs to engage in donation drives and to coordinate with local organizations that provide emergency food and supplies, such as food banks and nonprofit organizations. The American Red Cross is another good resource for homeless shelters to collaborate with during disasters (Soltani et al., 2015). The American Red Cross has access to supplies, trained volunteers, and other resources that can supplement the needs of the homeless shelter during a disaster.

Finally, redundancy in the homeless shelter's communication system is created by having multiple forms of communication available (cell phones, Internet, landline phone, walkie-talkies), and by training employees in how to shift between communication systems if one is disabled (Elachola, Al-Tawfiq, Turkestaini, & Memish, 2016). The contingency plans must be created before a disaster strikes, so that resources can be identified, the necessary relationships and agreements contracted, and so key stakeholders can be trained and can practice activating the contingency plans.

Tools and assessments. To assist a manager in creating contingency plans, disaster resilience indicator tools can be used. Disaster resilience indicator tools provide four data points for each critical function: (1) asset baseline condition (the current status/description of the asset), (2) spatial orientation of assets (where they are located), (3) methodology of the function (step-by-step process description), and (4) domain area descriptions (characteristics of the function/asset) (Cutter, 2016). As this information is collected, managers identify where possible disaster-based disruptions are likely to occur and what alternative options are available (van der Vegt, Essens, Wahlström, & George, 2015). To organize the contingency strategies created, it is important for the manager to develop some type of integrated system, such as a database, where contingency options can be stored and accessed when needed (Sahebjamnia et al., 2014).

In addition to assessing assets, it is also important to assess risks. The risk assessment procedure begins by identifying as many risks as possible that could impact the business (Knuth, Kehl, Hulse, & Schmidt, 2014). Step two is to research each risk for probability of occurrence, scope of impact, and severity of impact (Powell,

Mustafee, Chan, & Hammond, 2016). Step three is to prioritize the risks (Knuth et al., 2014). Prioritization can be based on likelihood to occur, scope of damage, severity of damage, or any other factor that is important to the organization. The outcomes of this assessment are then used to create a business impact assessment.

The business impact assessment (BIA) is used to predict the scope and severity of disruption a business will have to its critical functions if it experiences a disaster (Business Impact Analysis, 2017; Torabi, Soufi, & Sahebjamnia, 2014). The first step in conducting a BIA is to list the risks that were identified in the risk assessment and that are most likely to impact the organization (Torabi et al., 2014). Next, the manger will evaluate what type of impacts are likely to occur. To help with this evaluation, a business impact questionnaire form can be used (Appendix E). The information that is developed in this assessment will later be used to develop goals and objectives for helping the organization to recover from a disaster.

Writing a contingency plan. The depth of planning completed for a contingency plan depends on the complexity of the operations associated with a business. For homeless shelters, extensive functionality assessments will not be needed. However, it is still advantageous to examine a full-scale contingency plan to determine what elements are important to complete (Yamakawa & Cardon, 2017). The U.S. Department of Labor (2014) provides a useful template for an IT contingency plan. It is divided into six sections. Section one is the introduction. The introduction includes statements about the purpose, applicability, scope, and assumptions of the contingency plan, as well as subsections on references and recordkeeping (U.S. Department of Labor, 2014). The objective of this section is to establish the boundaries of the contingency plan, so employees know exactly when to implement it and when to use other strategies. In the second section, the content shifts to "Concepts of Operations" (U.S. Department of Labor, 2014). The sub-sections associated with this part of the contingency plan include a description of the critical function being addressed, a line of succession for managing the critical function during a disaster, and a list of roles and responsibilities for the employees responsible for the critical function. Section Three is the "Notification and Activation Phase" (U.S. Department of Labor, 2014). The objective of this phase of the plan is to provide directions on the plan's implementation. It includes directions on how to assess damage, how to assess alternative procedures, and how to activate the plan (U.S. Department of Labor, 2014). Section Four moves on to what the organization needs to do to recover from disaster-caused disruptions. It is organized by recovery goals and objectives (U.S. Department of Labor, 2014). The recovery goals are based on the findings from the business impact assessment conducted during the early stages of contingency planning. For example, a homeless shelter would have entries that look like this:

Recovery Goal 1: Call in appropriate experts to manage the stabilization and repair of the physical building.

> Manager: Call in experts to assess the physical structure and provide a quote.
>
> Board of Directors: Review repair quotes, authorize budget for recovery effort, and hire a contractor.

Section Five of the continuity plan helps the organization to "Return to Normal Operations" (U.S. Department of Labor, 2014). This section will identity what needs to be restored, how it is to be restored, and how to determine if the restoration was successful. Section Five also includes subsections for managing concurrent operations of critical functions at the temporary site and the home site, as well as instructions for deactivating the contingency plan (U.S. Department of Labor, 2014). The information presented in these sub-sections help employees to get the business operational again at the home site and to transition all operations and resources back to the home site. The final section is the "Plan Appendices" (U.S. Department of Labor, 2014). The appendices are a collection of information lists, policies, and memorandums covering how to contact key stakeholders and employers, service agreements, risk assessments, the Business Impact Analysis, and the continuity of operations plan. By completing this process, managers can quickly protect the business operations and maintain services for clients, as well as quickly transition between normal and crisis states without losing functionality or jeopardizing their relationship with customers. For homeless shelters, each section and sub-section should be developed, even if the development is only a few sentences or a referral to a different document or policy.

Strengths and weaknesses. Like building disaster resiliency, contingency planning is beneficial when done properly. According to Yamakama and Cordon (2017), the design of the contingency planning effort impacts how much value is created or lost by the process. For example, if the organization is effectively assessed and planning done to protect critical functions, then benefits can be expected to be reaped. The benefits include continuity of operation, fewer disruptions to business, and an easier and more cost-effective recovery (Yamakama & Cordon, 2017). However, when the people responsible for contingency planning do not do a good job or if they make common mistakes, then contingency plans can end up ineffective. The problems with ineffective contingency plans include impaired cost-efficacy and increased risks of disruptions to business during and after disasters (Yamakama & Cordon, 2017).

While the threat of an ineffective contingency plan is a threat that needs to be mitigated, managers that follow best practices for contingency planning processes can create many advantages for the organization. The first advantage is flexibility (Skipper, Hall, Hazen, & Hanna, 2014). Flexibility is an important trait to develop, as it allows managers to quickly shift between suppliers, transportation routes, communication channels, and even business strategies during disaster situations. The ability to shift to different tracks protects the company from shut downs and delays that can cost the operation time, money, reputation, brand value, and customers (Nejad, Niroomand, & Kuzgunkaya, 2014).

Another advantage of effective contingency planning is that it encourages managers to move away from transactional leadership and towards transformational leadership. Transactional leadership is short-term in its scope of perception and planning (Breevaart et al., 2014). Subsequently, it limits the ability of managers to plan for problems that will arise in the future and limits his/her ability to recognize the value of and justify engaging in disaster preparedness activities, such as contingency planning. Conversely, transformational leadership encourages managers to develop relationships with vendors and employees so that long-term interactions can be shaped and integrated into the company's operation strategy (Breevaart et al., 2014). The outcome of this shift is that managers engage in contingency planning and increases the ability of the organization to avoid short-term and long-term disruptions to operations.

One of the more tangible benefits offered by contingency planning is that it reduces losses (Sahebjamnia et al., 2015). This benefit alone is reason enough to engage in it, as good managers are interested in protecting organizational assets and revenues. This benefit is produced by minimizing disruptions to business operations, which for a homeless shelter would include taking in donations and delivering services to the homeless (Breevaart et al., 2014). It is also created by planning ahead to avoid damage to data, equipment, and other critical assets the organization needs to engage in business activities.

The final benefit offered by contingency planning to be discussed is psychological equilibrium. Psychological equilibrium means that employees and other stakeholders are able to remain calm and controlled during a disaster situation because of the planning that was done prior to the critical incident (Mole, North, & Baldock, 2017). Contingency planning does this by making stakeholders feel as if they are in control of the situation and by reducing unknowns. Psychological equilibrium of homeless shelter staff and volunteers is desirable, because it allows them to manage the crisis more effectively and helps to reduce the threat of secondary trauma (Nuttman-Shwartz, 2015). This benefit of contingency planning connects it to disaster resilience building, because reducing distress and promoting psychological equilibrium are outcomes both theories strive to achieve (Cavallo & Ireland, 2014; Cutter, 2013; Mole et al., 2017).

Emergency and Disaster Management Cycle

The emergency and disaster management cycle is made up of four phases. The phases are mitigation, preparedness, response, and recovery (Haddow et al., 2013). To improve disaster response outcomes, it is essential that all five phases be developed and completed effectively by organizations.

Phase one. The first phase of the emergency and disaster management cycle is the mitigation phase. During the mitigation phase, the disaster management team devises ways for improving the community's resilience and resistance to the impacts of future disasters and emergencies (Haddow et al., 2013). This may include such actions as passing new zoning restrictions on development in high-risk areas, retrofitting buildings to withstand hurricane or tornado conditions, or implementing preparedness programs to encourage local businesses to take responsibility for their own disaster preparedness and resiliency (Berke, Smith, & Lyles, 2012). Unlike the other phases in the emergency and disaster management cycle, the mitigation phase is ongoing instead of having a finite time period in which it is active. Disaster mitigation strategies are impacted by the Disaster Mitigation Act, which passed in 2000. The Disaster Mitigation Act mandated that any local, state, or tribal entity that receives federal grant money for disaster recovery and assistance to engage in disaster mitigation efforts to continue to qualify for this public assistance (Public Law 106-390).

Phase two. The second phase of the emergency and disaster management cycle is preparedness (Haddow et al., 2013). The first part of preparedness is planning. Planning involves most of the administrative work for disaster management, as it is when the disaster management infrastructure is developed, people are recruited, roles and responsibilities assigned, information gathered, and plans created (Haddow et al., 2013). When stakeholders in an organization decide to engage in disaster management, the initial step is to assemble a disaster management team. The size and diversity of the team depends on the organization and its needs and capabilities (Haddow et al., 2013). For example, a homeless shelter will likely assignment the manager the responsibility of completing all of the disaster preparedness tasks alone or with the help of volunteers with expertise in disaster preparedness. Conversely, large organizations, such as hospitals, need an interdisciplinary team made up of administrators, doctors, nurses, security staff, and experts from the community (Gowing, Walker, Elmer, & Cummings, 2017).

After the team is assembled, they are briefed on the emergency and disaster management process, and on what needs to be done to plan for disasters (Haddow et al., 2013). This briefing prepares the team to create an all-hazards disaster management plan, as recommended by FEMA (2017). The document that provides the theoretical foundation for this plan is the FEMA "Guide for All-Hazard Emergency Operations Planning" published in 1996. This guide explains why the plan is necessary, how it should be administered, who should be involved, and what it should include. The planning team should read through the guide in its entirety before moving on to the completion of the organization's all-hazards disaster preparedness plan.

The all-hazards disaster preparedness plan is divided into four main sections. Section one provides the introductory information to the plan, including a description of what the plan is, what policy authorized its utilization, accountability standards, and a signature page for key stakeholders in the organization (Nakanishi & Auza, 2015). This information is needed to integrate the all-hazards disaster preparedness plan into the organization's official policies and procedures. The second section of the plan is the main content of the document. This information will be applied to all disaster responses, and includes: a purpose statement, situation description and assumptions, a concept of operations statement, roles and responsibilities, administration and logistics considerations, a plan for developing and maintaining the plan, and a reference page (Nakanishi & Auza, 2015). The third section of the plan will be the Functional Annex Content. In this section, special tasks associated with disaster responses are planned for in detail (Nakanishi & Auza, 2015). Most organizations benefit from having functional annexes for direction and control, communications, warnings, emergency public information, evacuations, mass care, health and medical concerns, and resource management (Nakanishi & Auza, 2015). The final section of the all-hazards disaster preparedness plan is the annexes for specific hazards that require special disaster responses. For example, Nakanishi & Auza (2015) recommend the creation of annexes for hazards that cause mass damage and carnage, such as earthquakes, hurricanes, and tornados, as well as for hazards that require special responses, such as acts of terrorism, hazardous materials disasters, and radiological hazards. Another recommendation made by FEMA and other experts in disaster preparedness is to include planning annexes for populations with special needs (Dries et al., 2014; Hamann et al., 2016; Meyer, Vatcheva, Castellanos, & Reininger, 2015). Common special populations include non-speakers of English, people with disabilities, the elderly, children, and the homeless.

As a part of creating the all-hazards disaster preparedness plan, supportive planning and tasks need to be completed. For example, a risk assessment is completed to identify what risks pose a threat to the organization, contingency and continuity plans are created to ensure the organization can continue to operate during and after a disaster, and mutual aid agreements are made with neighboring jurisdictions to fill gaps in resources by agreeing to share, lend, and exchange resources when disasters strike (Murphy, Pearce, Chretien, & McLean-Purdon, 2017). These plans are referenced in the all-hazards disaster preparedness plan but are maintained separated or added to the plan as Appendices (Nakanishi & Auza, 2015).

After planning is complete, the plans are implemented to take actions to prepare the organization for a disaster. One task that is done during this phase is to collect and stockpile resources (Rebmann, Elliott, Artman, VanNatta, & Wakefield, 2016). The literature on preparedness and FEMA recommend having at least three days' worth of supplies on hand for a disaster response (Annis, Jacoby, & DeMers, 2016). Meeting this level of preparedness can be difficult for homeless shelters, because their supplies are donated and because when a disaster strikes, it is common for homeless populations to escalate during critical incidents, increasing the demand for services and supplies (Fogel, 2017). Therefore, the collection of disaster preparedness supplies will include finding partners, such as local churches and nonprofit organizations that can help with the overflow of homeless during a disaster response.

One of the most important tasks associated with the preparedness phase of the disaster management cycle is to train team members to put the various preparedness plans into action (Inglesby, 2011). Training can be carried out in several different ways. First, the team can be trained in a tabletop exercise in which the team reads a disaster scenario and then explains what each person needs to do to respond effectively to that scenario (Sandstrom, Eriksson, Norlander, Thorstensson, & Cassel, 2014). These exercises are easy to implement and low-costs, making them popular among small and medium enterprises. However, the drawback of the tabletop exercise strategy, is that the simulation is not realistic, which impacts the efficacy of the training. Ideally, training should simulate the conditions under which employees will be required to act when responding to a disaster. This makes full scale disaster response simulations necessary, even if they are only carried out one every one, two, three, four, or five years (Djalali et al., 2014). This type of simulation allows employees to practice their roles and responsibilities while the simulated disaster unfolds. This is advantageous because it tests employees' abilities to respond to changes in conditions while under stress. These full-scale simulations also identify systemic gaps and overlaps in preparedness (Djalali et al., 2014). For example, during a simulation, a homeless shelter may realize that where it stockpiles its disaster supplies makes them prone to damage from flooding. As problems are identified, the team will make notes and resolve them during their next planning and preparedness meeting.

Phase three. The response phase occurs once a critical incident occurs. A critical incident is a situation in which a hazard has impacted a community and has put the health and well-being of the community in jeopardy (Haddow et al., 2013).

The response phase involves activating the disaster plan, releasing resources, and stabilizing the situation. Once the emergency or disaster incident is stabilized, the fourth phase of the emergency and disaster management cycle is initiated, which is the recovery period. During this phase, it is important to have at least one person tracking resources so that the manager of the organization has a paper trail documenting who used what, for what purpose, at what time, and in what quantity (Haddow et al., 2013). Similarly, it is important for someone on the disaster management team to track communications (Steelman, Nowell, Bayoumi, & McCaffrey, 2014). The documentation of resource use and communications is important, because it provides data the team can use to evaluate the efficacy of the disaster response, to identity issues that need to be corrected, and to assess where problems developed or where possible fraud occurred.

Phase four. The next phase is the recovery period, which is when the community begins to rebuild and return to its post-incident condition (Haddow et al., 2013). The recovery period involves stabilizing the physical structures owned by the organization, relocating operations if needed, rebuilding structures, and restoring operations as quickly as possible. During the recovery period is also the time when resilience is tested (Cavallo & Ireland, 2014). To help promote resilience, the recovery period can be enhanced with the use of counselors to help employees and clients to work through their disaster-related stress and trauma so that long-term negative consequences can be avoided, such as Post Traumatic-Incident Stress Disorder (Brown, Beutler, Patterson, Bongar, & Holleran, 2016).

Crisis interventions also can be used to mitigate for disaster-related psychological problems (Boscarino, 2015). A good option for homeless shelters to use is psychological first aid, which can be implemented by anyone trained in this process. PFA is like regular first aid, in that its intent is not to treat injuries, but rather to stabilize victims of the crisis long enough to get them to the help they need (Hambrick, Rubens, Vernberg, Jacobs, & Kanine, 2014). The steps in the PFA model are:

- Make contact and engage victims of the disaster;
- Make sure the victims are safe and comfortable;
- Stabilize the victim by offering first aid as needed and helping them to calm down;
- Collect information from the victims about their immediate concerns and needs;

- Offer practical assistance;

- Help the victims to connect with their social support system;

- Disseminate information about how to cope with the stress and trauma of disasters; and

- Help the victims to connect with services they will need to recover from their disaster traumas. (McCabe et al., 2014).

Strengths and weaknesses. FEMA's emergency and disaster cycle (mitigation, preparedness, response, and recovery) is a valuable model. One advantage it offers is that it is simple in its design (Malilay et al., 2014). Anyone who is responsible for disaster preparedness can understand the model and its components. Additionally, the circular nature of the model's design promotes ongoing disaster preparedness efforts with the intent of making disaster preparedness a long-term process instead of an isolated activity (Malilay et al., 2014). The FEMA model for emergency and disaster management is also responsive to the size and traits of an organization. This means that the level of development of each phase in the cycle is under the control of the manager, allowing smaller companies to engage is less intense disaster preparedness efforts that larger more complicated firms (Malilay et al., 2014).

While the FEMA cycle for emergency and disaster management helps to focus managers on the basic tasks needed to promote disaster resilience and resistance to damage, the cycle has criticisms. The first criticism is that it is not intuitively circular. What this means is that the way in which FEMA presents its model can make some managers believe that disaster preparedness is linear and finite, instead of circular and infinite (Fekete, Hufschmidt, & Kruse, 2014). Subsequently, managers may make an initial effort to plan, prepare, and mitigate for disasters, but fail to monitor and update the disaster preparedness plans over time. This leads to outdated plans that are ineffective and do not cover added equipment, processes, and risks (Fekete et al., 2014). Another problem with the FEMA emergency and disaster management cycle is that FEMA promotes the cycle for governments and large organizations, while only promoting isolated planning and preparedness activities for small and medium organizations (Haddow et al., 2013). For example, governments and select organizations, such as hospitals, are required to engage in the full emergency and disaster management cycle and are given support for doing so. Conversely, small and medium enterprises (SMEs) are not encouraged to engage in the full cycle, but instead encouraged to complete a business continuity plan, contingency plans, and to build resilience (FEMA, 2017). While these tactics do mirror the emergency and disaster management cycle to some degree, the disconnectedness of the way in which the tactics are presented to SMEs limits managers' ability to understand the cycle, the order of its steps, and its circular and infinite nature. Subsequently, SMEs do not normally engage in effective disaster preparedness efforts, and even when they do, their outcomes are disappointing (Fogel, 2017; Medina, 2016).

All-Hazards Approach to Emergency and Disaster Management

Over the last century, the United States struggled with its development of a national emergency and disaster management strategy. Early strategies were ad hoc in nature, meaning that the government only got involved as a last resort. This led to huge financial, property, and casualty losses for the nation (Haddow et al., 2013). In the wake of the events of September 11, 2001, the United States Federal government took radical steps to improve the efficiency in how the nation responded to its emergencies and disasters.

After experimenting with a variety of disaster management models, the option selected for implementation on a national scale was the all-hazards model for emergency and disaster management (Haddow et al., 2013). This model provided a scalable infrastructure for managing any type of emergency or disaster that a community or state could face. The objective of this model was to standardize how governments managed disasters so that interjurisdictional collaborations were easy to accommodate when needed, and so that a community could minimize the amount of work needed to prepare for a disaster while maintaining a high level of preparedness (Haddow et al., 2013).

The all-hazards approach was adopted nationwide and proved itself to be an effective infrastructure for the average citizen of a community. However, where this model failed was in meeting the special needs of vulnerable populations, which are often not adequately planned for in the all-hazards model (Donahue, Cunnison, Balaban, & Sochats, 2012). While the all-hazards model recommended the creation of an addendum for special population planning and responses, governments either failed to do this or they failed to include representatives from special populations in planning, preparedness, response, recovery, and mitigation activities (Donahue et al., 2012). Subsequently, communities were not adequately prepared to help special populations at any phase of the emergency and disaster management cycle.

Strengths and weaknesses. The primary strength of the all-hazards approach to disaster preparedness is that it saves time, money, and resources (Haddow et al., 2013). Instead of planning for each risk separately, a main infrastructure is created that can be applied to and scale up or down to fit any emergency or disaster that occurs. Another strength associated with the all-hazards approach is that it makes disaster response and recoveries more efficient and effective (Hamer et al., 2017). Efficiency and effectiveness are enhanced by engaging in planning, preparedness, and mitigation efforts in advance of disasters. These pre-disaster efforts are important because they minimize losses and ensure that resources, roles, responsibilities, and procedures are clearly defined and allocated for response and recovery efforts, so they can be implemented or used immediately when needed (Hamer et al., 2017). Another advantage of the all-hazards approach to disaster preparedness is that it promotes the adoption of disaster preparedness as cultural value (Gregory, 2015). The all-hazards approach requires extensive planning and preparedness efforts that necessitate an on-going investment in the process. To support the ongoing demands of the all-hazards disaster preparedness process, the organization must integrate disaster preparedness as a cultural value (Gregory, 2015; Haddow et al., 2013). If organizations do not adopt this cultural value, then managers are not going to be authorized or encouraged to engage in the level of preparedness activities needed to develop and maintain an all-hazards preparedness strategy.

Despite the values added by the all-hazards approach, it has two primary problems. The first problem is that its design is ambiguous and generalized (Haddow et al., 2013). The objective of an all-hazards disaster preparedness plan is to provide an infrastructure that can be used for any critical incident, therefore, response details are largely missing from the plan (Llewellyn, Dominey-Howes, Vileneuve, & Lewis-Gargett, 2016). For example, the plan will state that supplies are needed, but will not specify what supplies are needed, in what quantity, how and where they are to be stored, and how they are to be managed between disasters. Additionally, the generalized nature of the planning and preparedness efforts neglects the preparedness needs of special populations, such as the homeless, elderly, children, people with disabilities, and non-native speakers of English (Haddow et al., 2013). Subsequently, the preparedness plans created by local and state governments often under-plan or fail to plan for special populations, leaving the special populations responsible for their own disaster preparedness.

The second problem associated with the all-hazards approach to emergency and disaster management is that to be effective, a competent leader is needed to head the effort (Gregory, 2015). To be an effective leader for an all-hazards disaster preparedness team, the person needs to have knowledge of the emergency and disaster management cycle, be good at building relationships, have KSAs in team building, be competent in conflict resolution, and have good interpersonal communication skills (Haddow et al., 2013). Unfortunately, most people who lead disaster preparedness in an organization are assigned the responsibility despite them not having any training or KSAs in disaster management or group leadership (Gregory, 2015). These deficits impair the efficacy of the all-hazards preparedness team.

Holistic Planning

Part of the all-hazards approach to disaster management is to develop a holistic planning team during the planning phase of the disaster management cycle (Haddow et al., 2013). Holistic planning simply means that the planning involves representatives from a cross section of the community (Fakhruddin & Chivakidakom, 2014). In most cases, the holistic planning team includes representatives from the community's department of emergency and disaster management, the local government, the state government, first responder agencies, the local medical industry, and possibly local companies (Fakhruddin & Chivakidakom, 2014; Raju & Becker, 2013). In the United States, the holistic planning team also likely involves local politicians and notable residents of the community.

However, as the earlier discussion on disaster management revealed in the introduction, holistic planning teams are not including representatives from special needs populations, such as the homeless (Fakhruddin & Chivakidakom, 2014) The oversight of not recruiting representatives from special needs populations in a community means that the needs of special populations are not adequately addressed in planning, preparedness, response, recovery, and mitigation activities.

Strengths and weaknesses. The main advantage produced by holistic planning is that it increases the tangible and intangible resources a disaster preparedness team has at their disposal (Fakhruddin & Chivakidakom, 2014). The more diverse the preparedness team is, the more comprehensive the risk assessment and planning documents will be. However, with diversity comes many problems. The first problem is incompatible personalities and ideologies (Ehrke, Berthold, & Steffens, 2014). In planning for disaster preparedness, personality and ideology difference emerge when different groups are brought into the planning team. For example, when a homeless shelter is creating its disaster prepared plans, the local government representatives may have priorities that they want the preparedness plan to address that have political significance, while the homeless shelter manager may have a different set of priorities that are based on practical needs of clients during a disaster situation. The second problem is that recruiting a diverse team may prove to be impossible (Fakhruddin & Chivakidakom, 2014). This is particularly true of nonprofit organizations, such as homeless shelters, that may have limited support from the community (Lee & Fleming, 2015).

Studies on Disaster Preparedness

To build a solid understanding of what is already known about disaster preparedness, as it relates to the population of American homeless, three sub-topics are important to review. The first topic is the core competencies for disaster preparedness. This topic examines disaster preparedness practices generally to identify key knowledge, skills, and abilities (KSAs) that improve preparedness outcomes. The second topic is studies of homeless-focused disaster preparedness, which reviews the application of disaster preparedness practices to homeless populations, studies of disaster preparedness efficacy, and analyses of other issues related to disaster preparedness for the homeless. The final topic is studies of other populations and their relationship to disaster preparedness. This topic covers efficacy, case, and comparison studies. The information reviewed, identifies concepts, practices, and things to avoid that can be used by the current study to evaluate the depth of preparedness engaged in by the sampled homeless shelters during the Level B data analysis.

Studies of core competencies for disaster preparedness. When screening the literature on core competencies for disaster preparedness, multiple themes emerged. The first theme was that disaster preparedness education needed to be standardized to ensure core competencies were developed in every organization. Cranmer and Biddinger (2014) support this recommendation in their study of the professionalization of disaster preparedness. The recommended process involved identifying the core competencies for effective disaster preparedness and to then train all disaster preparedness planning teams in these KSAs. Adams, Canclini, and Frable (2013) also supported the need for standardized education for people involved in the disaster management cycle. Adams et al. (2013) conducted a case study of emergency preparedness education for nurses, who are essential players in disaster responses. The findings from this study revealed that core competencies for disaster preparedness need to be integrated into professional education programs to promote consistency in the application of disaster preparedness best practices, and to continuously monitor and update core competencies to ensure professionals have the right KSAs (Adams et al., 2013). Rafferty-Semon, Jarzembak, and Shanholtzer (2017) added to the

Adams et al. (2013) findings by further promoting the use of Point of Distribution/Dispensation (POD) as a training tool for disaster preparedness core competencies.

A POD is a logistical planning tool that is created through the efforts of a collaboration between local health departments, FEMA, and other associated organizations (Rafferty-Semon et al., 2017). It helps to coordinate inter-agency preparedness and responses to disasters. This practice establishes two new core competencies in disaster preparedness. The first is logistical planning and the second is collaborating. Logistical planning is facilitated by various planning documents, such as the POD, business continuity plan, contingency plans, and a disaster preparedness plan (FEMA, 2017; Rafferty-Semon et al., 2017). Each of these plans identify resources and their locations, and assign roles and responsibilities related to acquiring, managing, and putting into use designated resources during a disaster response. These plans not only prepare the organization for a disaster response, but they are also useful in making collaborations possible. The reason is that the various logistical plans clarify who is responsible for what resource or service during the disaster response, who will oversee the resources used, and how accountability for the use of resources will be maintained (Adelaine, Shoaf, and Harvey, 2015). Another reason why the logistical plans are important to disaster preparedness collaborations is that address the main barriers identified in the study by Adelaine et al. (2015), ability to communicate, personnel issues, and finances. The written document makes communication easier because the documents include communication plans and clear instructions about the collaborations; and personnel and finance gaps are filled by combining the resources of multiple organization. The challenge that remains, however, is that research by Jahre, Pazirandeh, and Wassenhove (2016) shows that "despite the increased attention, there is no unified understanding across organizations about what constitutes logistics preparedness and how it can improve operations" (p. 372).

Another core competency identified in the literature on disaster preparedness is risk reduction. Birnbaum, Daily, O'Rourke, and Loretti (2015) demonstrated in their study that a risk-reduction framework is needed to promote effective disaster preparedness. This framework has 14 elements and is based on the Disaster Logic Model (DLM). The 14 steps are:

> (1) hazards and risks identification; (2) historical perspectives and predictions; (3) selection of hazard(s) to address; (4) selection of appropriate indicators; (5) identification of

current resilience standards and benchmarks; (6) assessment of the current resilience status; (7) identification of resilience needs; (8) strategic planning; (9) selection of an appropriate intervention; (10) operational planning; (11) implementation; (12) assessments of outputs; (13) synthesis; and (14) feedback. (Birnbaum et al., 2015, p. 309).

These elements are applied to the disaster preparedness process at several points, making the process multidirectional.

Risk management is cyclic in disaster preparedness and applies to all five steps in the disaster management process. For example, in preparedness, risk management is used to identify risks; in planning, it is used to understand what threats and risks to plan for; in mitigation, the risk management framework is used to identify standards/benchmarks to achieve in safety and security; in disaster response, the framework instructs managers to monitor for how well mitigation efforts worked; and in the disaster recovery phase, the framework instructs managers to address any problems identified during the response so that new risks/threats can be identified and mitigated (Birnbaum et al., 2015).

The literature reviewed also identified interdisciplinary functionality as a core competency for disaster preparedness. Gallardo, Djalali, Foletti, and Ragazzoni (2015) established this core competency in their systemic review of literature on "Core Competencies in Disaster Management and Humanitarian Assistance" (p. 430). The studies reviewed by Gallardo et al. (2015) consistently promoted the need for cross-sectorial and interdisciplinarity when engaging in each stage of the emergency and disaster management cycle. The reason was that disaster preparedness activities require a wide range of KSAs that extend beyond just a single discipline or sector (Gallardo et al., 2015). For example, the study by Burke, Lyznicki, and James (2012) presented that public health disaster preparedness requires knowledge in medicine, logistics, risk management, business administration, industrial/organizational psychology, and disaster management.

The final disaster preparedness core competency to be discussed is the ability to prepare clients served by an organization before a disaster occurs. This competency is important, because unprepared clients, particularly special needs clients, consumer higher quantities of time and resources provided by disaster response teams (Heagele, 2016). This is a disadvantageous position to be in, because it makes it more difficult for low-resource organizations, such as homeless shelters, to meet the needs of their clientele. However, preparing the homeless for disasters is much more difficult than preparing clients from other populations in the United States.

Homeless-focused studies. Homelessness is a problem shared by most nations. From rural communities to urban metropolises, a proportion of each population is likely to experience homelessness at some point (Persson & Povitknia, 2017). The ability to respond to the special needs of the homeless is highly dependent on the disaster preparedness engaged in by organizations that serve this population, as well as the politics governing societies. Persson and Povitkina (2017) hypothesize that "democratic institutions are insufficient for securing protection from disasters in contexts of corruption, poor planning, and public administration incompetence" and that "the effect of democracy on the extent of human suffering in disasters is contingent on the ability of governments to implement their tasks or the quality of implementing institutions" (p. 833). When this hypothesis is tested, Persson and Povitkina (2017) reveal that democracy does help to improve the efficacy of disaster preparedness; however, this strength is eliminated if bureaucratic inefficacies and political gameplay corrupts the system. Managers of homeless shelters, therefore, need to understand what possible systemic inefficacies exist in their local community political system, so that the they can mitigate for these problems.

In addition to understanding the political barriers to effective disaster preparedness, managers of homeless shelters also need to assess other vulnerabilities and hazards. Walters and Gaillard (2014) conducted a study on the vulnerabilities and hazards of being a marginalized population. The researchers reveal through their data that marginalized populations, such as the homeless, are more apt to suffer longer than other populations post-disaster because they do not have access to sufficient resources to protect them from hazards posed by disasters or to recover effectively from a disaster (Walters & Gaillard, 2014). Additionally, since the homeless are more exposed to the elements, they are more likely to suffer health-related problems during common crises, such as extreme summer weather. For example, a study by Nicolay, Brow, Johns, and Ialynytchev (2016) shows that homeless are highly susceptible to heat related illnesses during extreme summer critical incidents, mainly because of a lack of understanding of the risks posed by heat exposure and when to seek help. Nicolay et al. (2016) recommended utilizing mobile medical care and shelters to mitigate for risks posed against the homeless during heat-related disasters. This policy could also be used for educating the homeless about other disaster preparedness KSAs that they need to develop. Fogel (2016) reinforces the need for this type of disaster preparedness strategy with the findings from a focus group study.

The study shows that homeless people are not adequately informed about disaster response services offered by local governments, including where disaster shelters are located, where to connect with free transportation to the disaster shelters, and where to access other resources to help them before, during, and after a disaster.

Not surprisingly, the organizations charged with managing the needs of the homeless during and after a disaster are homeless shelters. While a logical choice based on who connects most effectively with the homeless, these organizations face multiple barriers to effective disaster preparedness for their clientele. According to a study presented by Gin, Kranke, Saia, and Dobalian (2016), two factors created the most problems for homeless shelter disaster preparedness. The first problem is that representatives from homeless shelters are not usually included in community disaster preparedness activities (Gin et al., 2016). Subsequently, the community does not know what needs exist and homeless shelters do not know what resources and services will be offered by the community during a disaster. This problem makes serving the homeless during and after a disaster difficult. The second problem identified by Gin et al. (2016) was "barriers to postdisaster services" (p. 1). Like other nonprofit organizations, recovery grants and loans are not readily available. The federal government prioritizes resources to individual households and to organizations that contribute to local economies and their revenue bases (Gin et al., 2016). The government devalues homeless shelters during recovery, because (1) clientele do not have physical addresses so they cannot apply for assistance, (2) clientele does not generate any tax revenue for local economies, and (3) homeless shelters do not generate revenue for local economies, beyond small payroll tax contributions (Gin et al., 2016). The recommendations made by Gin et al. (2016) to correct for these problems are to enact a multisector effort involving stakeholders in homeless shelters to improve the organizations' access to resources, to improve the diversity of their disaster preparedness planning efforts, and to enhance the overall quality of disaster planning and preparedness that takes place.

When engaging in disaster preparedness for the homeless, it is important to consider the unique strengths this population has for surviving. Unlike most of the population, every day is like a disaster for the homeless, as they are without electricity, housing, food, and access to resources that the average person takes for granted (Vickery, 2015). Since people without homes must manage these challenges daily, they have unique strategies for surviving during difficult times. For example, in a case study by Settembrino (2017), homeless men were studied regarding their ability to mitigate for natural hazards and risks. The results showed that this population utilized social networks to find shelter and resources, such as asking friends if they can stay with them during the disaster period (Settembrino, 2017). The disaster risk mitigation strategies developed by the homeless need to be communicated to the disaster preparedness teams, both at the organization level and at the government level, this is called upstream disaster management (Sundareswaran, Ghazzawi, & O'Sullivan, 2015). This practice should enhance the efficacy of disaster preparedness for the homeless.

    The final sub-topic to be discussed relating to homeless-focused studies is special concerns. One special concern identified was that disaster damage can increase homelessness rates. For example, in the study by Doran et al. (2016), showed that highly destructive disasters, such as Hurricane Sandy, not only increase the demand for emergency room care for people who were homeless prior to the disaster, but also for people who lost their homes during the disaster (Doran et al., 2016). Kar (2016) also explained that post-disaster homelessness hits older populations harder than younger populations, because older adults have more limited access to resources. Subsequently, while younger adults have income and social resources to use post-disaster, older adults are less likely to have these resources and are more dependent on social services provided by the government, nonprofit organizations, and homeless shelters (Kar, 2016). The observations made by Doran et al. (2016) and Kar (2016) increase the importance of disaster preparedness among homeless shelters. Another special concern identified by the literature was pets owned by the homeless. In the study by Thompson et al. (2014), the refusal of a disaster shelter or homeless shelter to accept pets discouraged many homeless from using the shelters. For the homeless, pets are a valuable asset that provide emotional support, companionship, and security (Thompson et al., 2014). If homeless shelters want to prepare effectively for the protection of their clientele, then planning for pets needs to be included in the preparedness process.

Studies of other populations. The first population reviewed was healthcare providers. This population was commonly used as a subject of disaster preparedness research, because communities had a heightened need for healthcare services during and after disasters (Tosh et al., 2014). Because the government viewed healthcare as a critical function of society, it set regulations that required healthcare providers to create and implement disaster preparedness plans to protect customers and to promote business continuity (Walsh, Craddock, Gulley, Strauss-Riggs, & Schor, 2015).

The first practice used by healthcare providers to prepare for disasters was the use of health care coalitions (HCCs). Healthcare systems developed HCCs to promote community and organization-level disaster preparedness and resilience (Walsh et al., 2015). When evaluated, HCCs were shown to offer the following benefits: interdisciplinary partnership building, the creation of a forum that promotes capacity building of a community, and a platform for promoting effective inter-agency communications. Despite these benefits, however, HCCs were also shown to have issues, including problems with engaging stakeholders, education and training struggles, standardization of processes and procedures, and conflicts of interest (Walsh et al., 2015). These problems were not limited to HCCs, as research conducted on healthcare organizations showed they also existed at the organization level of healthcare companies.

An example of the problem of the lack of standardized processes and procures was seen in the study by Agboola, Bernard, Savoia, and Biddinger (2015). This study targeted healthcare providers with the intent of evaluating the application of a three-part tool kit for measuring the performance of a collection of health emergency response exercises. The tool kit included (1) a database of assessment measures, (2) a tool for standardized data collection, and (3) a program outlining how to use the toolkit to evaluate various performance factors (Agboola et al., 2015). The results from the assessment revealed that 93% of the participants found the toolkit useful in "gauging their organization's performance during the exercise," and 79% viewed the toolkit as more effective than other performance measurement practices they used in the past (Agboola et al., 2015, p. 503). The lesson taken from this study was that it is important to have a formal strategy developed for measuring the performance of each disaster preparedness practice adopted by a homeless shelter.

Lane and McGrady (2016) extend the discussion started by Agboola et al. (2015) by exploring the need for emergency preparedness standards. The design of this study involved surveying 611 nursing homes located in North and South Carolina about their disaster preparedness activities and comparing the results to the preparedness recommendations promoted by the U.S. Department of Health and Human Services (Agboola et al., 2015). The results from this study shows that nursing homes in the two states surveyed are improving their disaster preparedness practices, but that significant gaps remain between what is being done and what experts recommend. This model validates the methodology selected for the current study of homeless shelter disaster preparedness as being appropriate, as well as demonstrates the value of the information derived from such a study in helping to address the disaster preparedness issues associated with organizations serving vulnerable populations.

The lack of effective training and education also creates barriers to effective disaster preparedness for healthcare providers. In a study of nurses conducted by VanDevanter et al. (2017), ineffectual education and training is noted by the nurses surveyed as one of the factors that inhibited their ability to respond to the threats posed by Hurricane Sandy and the subsequently hospital evacuation. This indicates that training of employees is an important part of disaster preparedness.

In addition to healthcare providers, the elderly are also frequently studied relating to their preparedness for disaster. The elderly are studied because they are more vulnerable to "adverse outcomes of disasters" than younger populations (Asjoda, Robinson, Gay, & Ramirez, 2015, p. 2117). In a study by Asjoda et al. (2015), for example, strategies for motivating elderly populations to prepare for disasters were investigated. In this study, the researchers revealed that it was important for the preparedness process for the elderly to involve social elements, including creating a relationship with the elderly and getting family, friends, and neighbors involved in preparing the elderly community members for a disaster (Asjoda et al., 2015). In application to preparing the homeless for a disaster, the two lessons learned are to create a relationship with the vulnerable population and to utilize community members to connect with and help prepare vulnerable populations for disasters.

Another population that is important to study is employees of the Veterans Health Administration. This organization provides services to veterans, who make up the majority of the homeless population (U.S. Department of Housing and Urban Development, 2016). This means that the preparedness that VHA employees have for disasters impacts their ability to serve veterans and their special needs, regardless if they are homeless or housed. In a study by Claver, Wyte-Lake, and Dobalian (2015), primary care providers working with the VHA home-base primary care (HBPC) program were interviewed about patient disaster preparedness. Themes found by the researchers include a lack of standardization for disaster preparedness among HBPC programs, training for practitioners participating in the program for disaster preparedness was limited or missing, and the HBPC programs placed responsibility for disaster preparedness on clients (Claver et al., 2015). These themes show that vulnerable populations are unreasonably expected to be self-sufficient in disaster preparedness, even though they are dependent on service providers for meeting their everyday needs. This is an oversight that needs to be corrected by shifting responsibility for disaster preparedness for vulnerable populations, such as the homeless, to service providers.

A related population to the VHA employees is military personnel, veterans, and their dependents. It is assumed that since military members and their families are highly skilled at preparing for the challenges of military life, that they are equally skilled at preparing for and responding to disaster situations (Annis et al., 2016). To test this assumption, Annis et al. (2016) conducted a survey study of U.S. Navy personnel and veterans living in the San Diego metropolitan area. To assess their level of preparedness, the survey established if the respondents met the FEMA standards for recommended preparedness, including having three days' worth of food, water, medication, and other necessary supplies. The results from this study showed that the military sample was no more prepared for disasters than the general public (Annis et al., 2016). This indicates that it should not be assumed that homeless vets have the KSAs needed to be self-sufficient in disaster preparedness.

Finally, sex differences in disaster preparedness practices are important to study to identify where strengths and weaknesses exist. Reyes and Lu (2017) tackle the topic of women's vulnerability during disasters in their study. The women studied came from the Philippines, where socioeconomic stratification disadvantages women more than men. The results show that disaster preparedness is more difficult for women in cultures that are dominated by men, because women are dependent on men to provide them with access to resources, information, and power to act (Reyes & Lu, 2017). The concern this raises for the current study is that women who are homeless are highly likely to be the victims of domestic violence/abuse and to have children with them (Song, Wenzel, Kim, & Nam, 2017). Subsequently, homeless shelters need to adopt disaster preparedness strategies that address the unique needs of disadvantaged demographic groups, such as abused women and children.

Summary

The United States utilizes an all-hazards approach to disaster management (Haddow et al., 2013). This approach involves the creation of a holistic disaster management team, which creates a scalable disaster management plan that can be used to manage any type and any size of emergency or disasters. The problem with that the all-hazards model creates, however, is that it fails to plan for the special needs that the community's vulnerable special populations have (Gin et al., 2015). This failure is due in large part to the fact that representatives from the community's special populations are not a part of the community's holistic disaster management team. The holistic disaster management team instead assumes that the service providers for the homeless will be responsible for learning what assistance is available and for conducting organization-level disaster planning and preparedness (Every & Thompson, 2014). While the service providers do engage in their own preparedness and disaster management planning efforts, their efforts are less effective because of a disconnect between these agencies and the community's holistic disaster management team. To understand the severity of the problems created by the disconnection between service providers for the homeless and community disaster preparedness, it is first necessary to understand what best practices are recommended by the service providers for the homeless. The best practices recommended by the service providers will establish what community-level holistic disaster management teams need to incorporate into their own planning efforts and documents to enhance the efficacy of the community's response to the special needs of the homeless in disaster management.

CHAPTER THREE: METHODOLOGY

This study addressed the problem of the failure of official emergency and disaster systems to plan for the special disaster preparedness needs of the homeless (Coe et al., 2015). In response to the identified problem, the purpose of the study was to assess the gaps in disaster preparedness that existed for the homeless in the United States and to determine the vulnerabilities that the gaps created. Four research questions guided the investigation and analysis.

RQ1: What are the best practices recommended by experts in managing the special needs of the homeless in regard to the emergency and disaster management processes of Mitigation, Preparedness, Response, and Recovery?

RQ2: What disaster preparedness steps are addressed by homeless shelters and other disaster service providers for the homeless?

RQ3: What gaps exist between best practices recommended by FEMA and other disaster preparedness experts and what homeless shelters and other disaster service providers for the homeless are currently doing regarding emergency and disaster preparedness planning?

RQ4: What vulnerabilities are created by the gaps in disaster preparedness planning for the homeless in the United States?

The answers to these questions were mined from disaster preparedness plans and policies using a qualitative content analysis, as well as by the construction of GIS maps that illustrated the overlaps of where disasters were declared in states and where the state's homeless shelters were clustered. The following chapter provides a detailed description of the research methodology, including a description of the research methodology and design, population and sample used, materials and instruments utilized, operational definitions of variables, measurements, study procedures, data collection and analysis processes, assumptions, limitations, delimitations, ethical considerations and assuredness, and finally, a summary of the chapter.

Research Methodology and Design

A four-part research process was used. The first component was a content analysis of best practices, as defined by FEMA and other disaster preparedness organizations/experts, and disaster preparedness planning practices executed by homeless shelters in the United States. The second part of the study's design was a gap analysis, in which actual disaster preparedness planning practices were compared to best practices to identify gaps in preparedness behaviors. The third part of the research design was a spatial data analysis that utilized GIS technology, FEMA disaster declaration data, and homeless shelter directories for each state. This analysis evaluated if homeless shelters were significantly impacted by disaster declarations. The final component of the research design was the application of triangulation between the literature review case studies, content analysis, gap analysis, and spatial data analysis. This process assessed if the data collected indicated potential correlations between gaps identified and case study issues relating to how the homeless were supported during disaster responses, as well as to assess what level of disaster preparedness planning was necessitated by actual disaster risk rates for homeless shelters.

Part I: Content analysis. The research design selected for the current study was a content analysis. Content analyses are unique because they can be viewed as either an intersection between qualitative and quantitative research or primarily qualitative (Vaismoradi, Turunen, & Bondas, 2013). For the purposes of the current study, the content analysis focused on the qualitative concepts within the sampled documents, making it a qualitative study (Neuendorf, 2016). For example, I collected sample documents, read through them, identified themes, analyzed the patterns of themes, inferred what meaning was created by what was included in a document and how those elements were related to each other, and then compared the results from the best practice group to the current practice group to identify gaps and overlaps (Vaismoradi et al., 2013).

    The analysis of the data collected for a content analysis can be structured using various methodologies. The possible methodologies are a structuralist analysis that examines the structure of how the identified elements are related to each other to produce meaning; an interpretist analysis that examines how theory is created from how the content in the document is organized; and rhetorical analysis that focuses on how the information is presented more so than what is said (Neuendorf, 2016). For the purposes of this study, the analysis used was the structuralist approach. This approach was selected because the study wanted to establish the structure of disaster preparedness best practices so that gaps in compliance among homeless shelters could be assessed (Balzacq, 2015). The structuralist analysis dissects media to see what elements are used to create the final product, and to establish what function each component of the document plays (Schreier, 2014). The structuralist approach also was cited in the literature as being an effective option, because it was easy to apply to digital documents and to abstract out elements that can later be used to produce predictive or descriptive algorithms (Ignatow, 2016).

The content analysis is an appropriate methodology because the topic under investigation, disaster preparedness for the homeless, is relatively unstudied. The content analysis, therefore, served three purposes. First, it identified the theoretical framework for disaster preparedness best practices, as defined by experts in the field of disaster management; second, it identified themes in what disaster preparedness planning homeless shelters completed; and finally, it provided a structure for comparison so that gaps in compliance with best practices in disaster preparedness planning could be conducted in a later phase of the study (Neuendorf, 2016). The findings from this part of the content analysis produced the answer for research question number one, "What are the best practices recommended by experts in managing the special needs of the homeless in regard to the emergency and disaster management processes: Mitigation, Preparedness, Response, and Recovery?

The application of the structuralist approach to the current content analysis involved two steps. Step one was to collect documents produced by authorities on disaster preparedness for general populations, such as FEMA (2017), and disaster preparedness for homeless populations, such as the HUD Exchange (2017). The documents sampled included templates and guides for disaster preparedness produced by experts in emergency and disaster management, as opposed to general discussions or studies of disaster preparedness practices. A content analysis of these documents identified themes in best practices for preparedness, and subsequently created a framework for what homeless shelters and other disaster service providers should be doing to prepare to serve the homeless during an emergency or disaster.

The second part of the content analysis identified the themes in disaster preparedness found in preparedness policies and plans created by homeless shelters and other organizations that delivery disaster services to the homeless in the United States. Disaster preparedness plans were collected from the Internet and analyzed for themes in preparedness activities, such as forming a preparedness committee, creating contingency plans, and identifying resources (Every, 2016). As themes emerged, categories were created to organize the data. Additionally, as new agencies were identified as having responsibilities to prepare to serve the homeless during a disaster response, those agencies were sampled, and their disaster preparedness plans analyzed. The findings from this part of the content analysis answered research question number two, "What disaster preparedness steps are commonly addressed by homeless shelters and other disaster service providers for the homeless?"

The value the content analysis added to the study was that it established two things. First, it established best practices in disaster preparedness planning, as defined by experts in disaster management. Best practices are the activities that experts recommend organizations engage in to prepare for a disaster to minimize damage, to protect assets, and to promote a quicker and more efficient recovery (Adams, Prelip, Glick, Donatellow, Eisenman, 2017). Second, it established trends in what homeless shelters are doing to plan and prepare for disasters. These two findings not only described the best and current practices, but they were also used to identify gaps in homeless shelter adherence to best practices for disaster preparedness planning in the gap analysis portion of the study.

In support of the use of a content analysis for the current study, the high level of validity associated with this methodology is noted. Validity means that what is measured is what is intended to be measured (Neuendorf, 2016). Internal validity is created by aligning conceptual and operational definitions of variables selected for the study (Neuendorf, 2016). For example, in the current study, the variable being measured is disaster preparedness. This variable is conceptualized as the collection of planning and mitigating efforts engaged in by an organization with the intent to be prepared to manage the challenges posed by an emergency or disaster, and the associated operational definition is the completeness of planning and mitigating for emergencies and disasters (Johnson, 2014). External validity is addressed by examining the generalizability of the results to other settings (Neuendorf, 2016). In the current study, external validity was constructed by establishing best practices for disaster preparedness, which are universal in nature, and using these best practices to determine if organizations that serve the homeless are using the best practices and to what degree (Wyte-Lake, Claver, Dalton, & Doblian, 2015). In support of the generalizability of the findings and measures of the content analysis for this study, the best practices established can also be used to assess compliance rates of any sector's disaster preparedness, not just organizations that serve the homeless.

    In selecting the content analysis methodology for the current study, other quantitative and qualitative study designs were deemed to be inappropriate or less effective for achieving the study's goals and objectives. First, all other quantitative designs were ruled out for this study because the research questions needed to be answered with some inclusion of qualitative descriptions instead of numerical measurements (Bernard, 2017). Second, qualitative study designs remained contenders, however, each remaining design failed to provide the structural objectivity that was offered by the content analysis option. For example, one option was a survey study in which a questionnaire would be administered to the target population. This option was ruled out because response rates to survey studies are low and because it would involve the implementation of additional IRB protocols to protect the human subjects studied (Bernard, 2017). Additionally, the analysis of the survey data would lack the reliability, objectivity, and validity associated with the content analysis. Another qualitative option considered was an interview study design. This option had time and resource requirements that made it impractical for the time frame available for the study. Finally, a case study design was considered but ruled out because it would not provide sufficient data to be useful by professionals in homeland security or social services (Bernard, 2017). The only option that was feasible in terms of time, resources, and practicality of design was the content analysis.

Part II: Gap analysis. A gap analysis is when current practices are compared to a baseline of expected or desired practices to determine where deficits in current practices exist (Le et al., 2017). This methodology is heavily used in the social sciences to determine gaps between policy and practice, between needs that exist, and needs being met, and between promises made by politicians and what is delivered by politicians (Mechler, 2016). In emergency and disaster management, gap analyses are commonly used to assess where improvements need to be made in the disaster management cycle (Mechler, 2016).

For the current study, the gap analysis compared the current practices identified in Part I of the study design to the best practices framework. This comparison identified gaps in preparedness, establishing where homeless shelter disaster preparedness practices need to be improved. These findings added value to the study by defining current practices deficits, so that later analyses could propose potential correlations between negative outcomes observed in past disaster responses with preparedness deficits, and to also assess if the deficits matter. A gap analysis is justified in this study because it is the most feasible way to answer research question number three, which asked, "What gaps exist between best practices recommended by FEMA and other experts and what homeless shelters and other service providers for the homeless are currently doing regarding emergency and disaster preparedness planning?"

The gap analysis was a viable study design because it has strong validity. This validity is created by comparing like items (Zhang & Wildermuth, 2016). For example, the current study compared disaster preparedness planning activities that are documented in disaster preparedness plans. Since what is intended to be measured was the difference between the best practices and current practices in disaster preparedness documentation, the right data was collected and measured. Reliability in the gap analysis is also enhanced by the nature of the gap analysis. For example, the best practice framework provides an objective structure to make comparisons against, and the current practices are provided. This means that findings from the gap analysis should be consistent regardless of who completes it.

Part III: Spatial data analysis. This part of the study design was selected to provide additional data to answer research question number 4, "How important is it for homeless shelters to have disaster preparedness plans in place?" The spatial data analysis utilized GIS technology to overlay state maps with information about where FEMA declared disasters between 2012 and 2017, and where homeless shelters were clustered in the state. The visual information produced by these integrated maps established the impact that disaster declarations have on homeless shelters. For example, if homeless shelters are clustered in the areas that are impacted regularly by disasters, then there is a heightened need for disaster preparedness, but if the homeless shelters are not located where disasters tend to occur in the state, then a lower level of disaster preparedness is needed.

The value of the information provided by the spatial data analysis was created by the relevancy and validity of the data, and the reliability of the analysis. To be relevant, the data selected needed to establish if disaster preparedness planning was needed for homeless shelters (Eidsvik, Mukerji, & Bhattacharjya, 2015). The data selected were disaster declaration locations and homeless shelter locations. These were valid variables because their proximity to each other impact how important and what degree of disaster preparedness planning is needed by homeless shelters. The reliability of the analysis of the data is also supported by the design of the spatial data analysis, because there are objective standards for drawing conclusions (Ghilani, 2017). For example, if no overlaps exist, then basic disaster preparedness is all that is needed, if a few overlaps exist then moderate disaster preparedness is needed and if there is complete overlap between where homeless shelters are located and where disasters are declared then an intensive level of disaster preparedness is needed.

Part IV: Triangulation. This component of the study design was essential in answering research question number four and establishing the significance of the findings from Part I, II, and III. This process involves the application of concepts and findings from the literature review, especially from the case studies reviewed, to the findings from the current study. The objective of this practice was to validate the findings, as well as to identify any new relationships or information that was not uncovered in prior studies. Triangulation was also used to interpret the meaning of the findings from the various parts of the study by comparing the different findings and extrapolating implications. Triangulation is a tool used by social science researchers to improve the reliability and validity of qualitative study designs, making it an important value-adding element of the overall study design (Zhang & Wildemuth, 2016).

Population and Sample

Four sets of data were used in the study. The first set of data, Dataset A, came from authorities on disaster preparedness. Some of the documents included the FEMA (2014) "Emergency Response Plan;' FEMA (2017) National Preparedness; the HUD Exchange (2017) information page for disaster preparedness for homeless populations, and the Public Health Emergency (2017) information page "Disaster Response for Homeless Individuals and Families: A Trauma-Informed Approach." The sample of best practices documents included eight unique documents. A convenience sample was taken, and the sampling criteria were that the document came from an expert in disaster preparedness and the expert developed a digital guide and/or template for organization level disaster preparedness. An APA bibliography was created for the best practices sample and stored to meet research documentation standards.

The second set of data, Dataset B, was disaster preparedness documents developed by homeless shelters. The sampling criteria were (1) a homeless shelter or other disaster service agency responsible for planning for the homeless created the document, (2) the organization was located in the United States, (3) a digital copy of the disaster preparedness plan was posted online, and (4) the document did not require passwords or special permission to access. The sample size for disaster preparedness plans for homeless shelters was originally 30 unique documents. However, during the content analysis, new agencies were identified and sampled, bringing the final sample size to 36. A convenience sampling technique was used in which a keyword search was used to identify homeless shelters and other disaster service providers for the homeless in the United States and to find their disaster preparedness plans. The first 36 disaster preparedness plans identified in the search results that meet the sampling criteria were printed out and all identification blacked out with a permanent marker to deidentify the source of the document. Additionally, as new agencies were identified in disaster preparedness plans, those agencies were also sampled and evaluated. A confidential list of URLs where the documents were found was created and stored to meet research documentation standards.

Dataset C was a collection of FEMA disaster declarations made by state for the years 2012 through 2017. The data came from the FEMA website and was public domain information. The data selected included when, where, and what type of disaster the declaration described. Sampling criteria for this dataset included a disaster declaration made between 2012 and 2017, and the locality had an organization sampled in Dataset B.

Dataset D was a list of homeless shelter addresses for the localities sampled in Dataset B and C. The addresses were sampled from online directories for homeless shelters. The information was publicly available.

Dataset A was used in Level A of the analysis and used to establish a baseline of best practices for disaster preparedness. Dataset B was used in both the Level A and Level B of the analysis. In Level A, Dataset B was compared to Dataset A findings to identify gaps and compliance in disaster preparedness, and in Level B, Dataset B was assessed for the depth and scope of disaster preparedness developed. Dataset C and D were then used to construct GIS maps to show where disasters were declared between 2012 and 2017, where homeless shelters are located in each state, and to establish if homeless shelters tend to be in high-risk zones for disasters or if they are outside of these high-risk zones. All four datasets were then used to determine what vulnerabilities the gaps in disaster preparedness created for the homeless in the sampled localities.

Materials and Instruments

The current study utilized Excel spreadsheets to document, organize, and analyze data. The first instrument was an Excel spreadsheet for best practices (Appendix A). Across the top of the spreadsheet was the following column headers: Strategic Theme, Source 1, Source 2….Source N, Mitigation, Preparedness, Response, and Recovery. Each row then described the strategic theme. The columns to the right of the theme included the code of 0 if this theme was not found in the column's source or a code of 1 if the theme was found in the column's source. Tallies of the values will be calculated for each row. An X was placed in the cell that correlates to the phase of the disaster management cycle the strategic theme applies to. Some strategic themes were associated with more than one phase of the disaster management cycle.

The second instrument created was for the current practices (Appendix B). The same basic format as the best practices spreadsheet was followed to make comparisons easier. Additional lines were added as new practices expanded upon the best practices list.

The third instrument was a checklist of best practice (Appendix C). In column 1 was a list of best practices. In column 2 was the coding for whether the best practice was observed in the current practices. The coding was 0 if the best practice item was not met and 1 if the best practice item was met.

The fourth instrument was the Level B analysis spreadsheet (Appendix D). In column 1 was a list of best practices that were identified in instrument 3 as being observed in current practices. In all the columns to the right of column 1 were the development ratings for each source. In the final column to the right, the development ratings for all the sources were averaged by best practice. The coding was a scale of one to ten, with one equating to superficially addressed, three being average engagement of the best practice, and five equating to full development of the best practice.

The final instrument used was GIS maps. ArcAgis GIS software and Google Earth were used to create state maps that showed where FEMA had declared disasters between 2012-2017. The locations of homeless shelters were also denoted on the maps.

Study Procedures

Step 1: Collect Dataset A and Dataset B. Documents associated with disaster preparedness were collected from two categories of sources. The first source of information was experts on the topic of disaster preparedness, such as FEMA and the authors of textbooks on Emergency and Disaster Management. The second source of information was homeless shelters and organizations that were responsible for disaster preparedness planning for the homeless.

Step 2: Identify best practices. Dataset A was assessed for best practices by screening each document and identifying the recommended steps and practices made by FEMA and other experts in disaster preparedness. The results were organized in a table by significance. The prevalence of the items found in the sampled Level A documents dictated the significance of the item.

Step 3: Identify current practices. The major steps in current practices for the disaster preparedness for the homeless came from the content of artifacts found in Dataset B. The identified practiced filled the cells in a table set up for identifying current practices. This table mirrored the layout found in Step 2.

Step 4: Conduct a gap analysis. This step involved comparing Dataset B results to Dataset A results. Gaps occurred when best practices were not found in any of the current practices artifacts. Gaps were noted.

Step 5: Assess the level of planning found in current practices. The disaster preparedness steps identified in Step 4 as being compliant with best practices from Dataset A were more deeply analyzed. The analysis described how the major step in the disaster preparedness process was completed, what it included, and what deliverables or actions resulted from the completion of the step. The level of development was then rated on a scale of 1 to 10.

Step 6: Report the results of the gap analysis. The results were summarized into several lists. List 1 identified the gaps in best practice compliance among current practices, List 2 identified the points of compliance current practices have with best practices, and List 3 detailed the development of each step found on List 2.

Step 7: Respond to gaps. An assessment of how well service providers for the homeless are preparing for disasters will be made, implications will be identified, and recommendations will be made. Mitigation strategies were developed for each item on List 1. These strategies were then discussed.

Step 8: Collect data for the spatial data analysis. The states, where disaster preparedness plans were sampled, were used to create List 4. This list was used to identify the states to sample for FEMA disaster declarations for 2012 through 2017. This information was collected from FEMA's website. List 4 was then used to sample the addresses of homeless shelters. Addresses were found online via publicly accessible directories, websites, and homeless shelter listings.

Step 9: Create GIS maps. ArcGIS software was used to construct GIS maps of each state sampled. The maps included information about where FEMA declared disasters between 2012 and 2017, and where homeless shelters are located in the state. A JPEG file was created and added to the study's report.

Step 10: Assess GIS maps. The information on the GIS maps was analyzed for relationships between disaster declarations and homeless shelter locations. Notations described where overlaps between disaster declarations and homeless shelters existed. Discussion of the implications of the overlaps identified concerning trends.

Step 11: Triangulate results. The findings from the gap analysis and the spatial data analysis were evaluated by comparing them to findings from the case studies found in Chapter Two. Case study findings from the literature review were used to identify implications about what the gaps identified mean for the homeless and the communities sampled, and what issues may be raised by the relationship between where disasters were declared and where homeless shelters are clustered. This step provided context for the findings.

Data Collection and Analysis

After collecting the documents and organizing them by type, best practices and current practices, the documents were analyzed for specific recommendations, strategies, and processes. Each strategic theme identified was entered into a spreadsheet which functioned as a tally sheet. The analysis of the data involved five steps. Steps one through three established general findings for current practices in preparedness for the homeless. This constituted Analysis Level A. Step one applied descriptive statistics, such as frequency and percentages, to identify what preparedness activities were considered best practices. The study defined a best practice as a concept or step promoted by an identified expert in disaster preparedness, such as FEMA. For current practices, strategies were listed according to their prevalence in the documents surveyed and prioritized from most prevalent to least prevalent. Step two of the data analysis created a checklist of best practices and determined to what degree organizations sampled were meeting the identified best practices. This was determined by identifying how many best practices each organization met. The frequencies of best practices met by each organization were then tallied and averaged. Current practices were considered as not meeting best practice if the average tally score was below .75 and was considered met if the score was at or above .75. Step three assessed what improvements were needed to fill in current practices gaps for disaster preparedness for the homeless. This step involved listing each missing best practice and identifying viable mitigation strategies for each missing step.

The second level of analysis, Analysis Level B, was also conducted. This part of the analysis evaluated the level of detail developed for each main step completed by the organization to prepare the homeless for disasters. Analysis Level B began by creating a list of the best practices identified as being used by the documents sampled. Each best practice was analyzed by sample to calculate a grade of completion of the best practice. The coding used a scale of one to ten, with one equating to superficially addressed, five being average engagement of the best practice, and ten equating to full development of the best practice. The scores for each best practice was tallied and averaged to determine what best practices need the most work and to determine the overall level of effort organizations serving the homeless are putting into their disaster preparedness.

The spatial data analysis required a visual assessment. This assessment described the relationships between where disaster declarations took place between 2012 and 2017 and where homeless shelters were clustered in the state. The objective was to determine if homeless shelters tended to be inside disaster-prone areas, outside of disaster-prone areas, or mixed between disaster and non-disaster-prone areas.

The final analysis involved triangulation between case studies discussed in Chapter Two, the results from the gap analysis, and the results from the spatial data analysis. Relationships, correlations, and deviations between findings were identified, described, and discussed. Then, implications and conclusions were drawn about what the findings suggest about disaster preparedness for the homeless.

Assumptions

The study assumes that homeless shelters and other agencies serving the homeless were responsible for disaster preparedness for the homeless population (Walters & Gaillard, 2014). It further assumed that local governments do not plan adequately for the homeless and their special needs during a critical incident (FEMA, 2017; Reininger et al., 2013). Finally, it assumed that multiple models for disaster preparedness were needed to create an adequate scope of best practices for disaster preparedness planning for homeless shelters and other disaster service providers for the homeless (FEMA, 2017; Paton, 2013).

Limitations

The most challenging limitation was that not all agencies that serve the homeless publish their disaster preparedness plans online. This limited what data was available. Additionally, most homeless shelters do not engage in disaster preparedness, which was a problem identified in the literature (Fogel, 2016; 2017). Additionally, a full disaster preparedness plan may not be published online, but a more developed plan may be kept on file by the organization. This could impact the gap analysis, however, based on other studies on homeless shelter preparedness, this is not a significant risk. Finally, the disaster preparedness plans that were available online may not be the latest version of the organizations' disaster preparedness plans. This also could impact the ability of the current study to define the current state of disaster preparedness for the homeless.

Delimitations

The study was limited to disaster preparedness in the United States. Also, to keep the study manageable, current practices documents were only be sampled from organizations that serve the homeless and who published their disaster preparedness plans online. No direct interviews with the homeless or organizations serving the homeless were conducted about what they do to prepare for a disaster.

Ethical Assurances

One concern of conducting research using the Internet was that ethical approval was not fully executed (Harriman & Patel, 2014). However, this study complies with Northcentral University's policies of social sciences research and went through the Internal Review Board analysis and approval process. This ensured that the study's design was ethical and did not violate any ethical standards held by NCU.

Another ethical concern was that informed consent does not take place when conducting research online (Harriman & Patel, 2014). The current study responded to this concern by only using documents that were publicly available. No direct interaction with people or organizations took place. This removes the need for informed consent (Connelly, 2014).

Finally, no identifying information was published or made available to third parties about where the data came from to protect the identities of the organizations whose disaster preparedness plans were studied. A hard copy of each disaster preparedness plan was made, all identifying information blacked out, the plans were filed using a lettered tab system, and the hard copies were stored in a locked cabinet. Additionally, a list of URLs and a digital copy of materials was kept on an encrypted USB jump drive, which was also stored in a fireproof safe.

Summary

The study was a structuralist qualitative context analysis of documents produced by service providers to the homeless that deal with the management of the special needs that the homeless have before, during, and after an emergency or disaster situation. The data collected came from government, non-profit, and private organizations that offered disaster preparedness and response services to the homeless. Eight unique American documents were collected for best practices in disaster preparedness and 36 unique documents were collected for American current practices in disaster preparedness for the homeless. The coding for the contextual analysis included creating nominal categories for each strategic theme identified in the documents collected and taking a ratio measurement of the frequency of each theme. Descriptive statistics identified which strategic themes were best practices and current practices. Best practices were defined recommendations made by experts in disaster preparedness, such as FEMA emergency preparedness templates. Current practices were defined as being any process mentioned in at least 70% of the current practices documents sampled. The current practices were compared to the best practices on two levels of analysis to determine where gaps exist and what changes were needed. The ultimate value of the findings from the current study was that awareness about the need to invest more effort into disaster planning, preparedness, and mitigation strategies for homeless populations will be created. The spatial data analysis evaluated the physical relationship between where disasters occurred in a state and where homeless shelters were positioned. Finally, triangulation between the literature review, gap analysis, and spatial data analysis was completed. This provided context for the findings from the current study, as well as helped to draw out implications about what the findings meant to homeless security, emergency and disaster management, disaster service providers for the homeless, and to the homeless populations in the United States.

Disaster Preparedness Planning for the Homeless

CHAPTER FOUR: FINDINGS

The purpose of the study was to assess the gaps between the best practices for disaster preparedness, as identified by FEMA and emergency and disaster management experts, and the current disaster preparedness activities completed by all organizations that offer disaster services to the homeless. Directing the assessment were four research questions, each focusing on one component of disaster preparedness for homeless populations. The four research questions were:

RQ1: What are the best practices recommended by experts in managing the special needs of the homeless in regard to the emergency and disaster management processes: Mitigation, Preparedness, Response, and Recovery?

RQ2: What disaster preparedness steps are addressed by homeless shelters and other disaster service providers for the homeless?

RQ3: What gaps exist between best practices recommended by FEMA and other experts and what homeless shelters and other disaster service providers for the homeless are currently doing regarding emergency and disaster preparedness planning?

RQ4: What vulnerabilities are created by the gaps in disaster preparedness planning for the homeless in the United States?

In this chapter, the data will be described in terms of its trustworthiness, primary sources and secondary source origination, and what findings were observed. The objective of the chapter is to present the data collected for the current research study and to connect it to the existing body of knowledge found in the literature review. The content of this chapter will include Trustworthiness of Data, Results, Evaluation of Findings, and Summary.

Trustworthiness of the Data

The challenge of conducting qualitative research was to collect trustworthy data. The trustworthiness of the data for the current study developed as the result of using several trusted methodologies. The first methodology used was data saturation. Data saturation is practice in qualitative research in which data is collected on a topic until clear trends in the data begin to repeat (Fusch & Ness, 2015). The verification of the trustworthiness of Dataset A involved this process. The objective of Dataset A was to establish best practices in disaster preparedness as applicable to organizations that deliver services to the homeless during a critical incident. Samples from experts in disaster preparedness were taken until data began to be repeated consistently. This limited the number of samples needed to establish the baseline for the gap analysis. Additionally, this process helped to establish the confirmability of the data, as showing the same practices and philosophies in multiple documents demonstrates the information came from the sources sampled and not from the researcher (Cope, 2014).

The second strategy used to ensure data trustworthiness was triangulation. Triangulation occurred when data collected was verified against the literature surveyed during the development of the research process, i.e. during the literature review (Fusch & Ness, 2015). The objective of the triangulation process was to promote dependability (Cope, 2014). Dependability means "the constancy of the data over similar conditions" (Cope, 2014, p. 89). Triangulation either verified that the new data supported existing findings, or that it deviated from existing findings. Trustworthiness emerged when alignments between findings exist, or when there was a definable reason why deviations existed. For example, the literature consistently reported that there was a lack of sufficient disaster preparedness activities taking place for the homeless, which supported the findings collected in Dataset B (Gin et al., 2016; Nicolay et al., 2016; Walters & Gaillard, 2014).

Reliability was another strategy implemented to protect the trustworthiness of the data. Reliability refers to the ability of external researchers to replicate the study based on the descriptions found in the methodology section (Tong & Dew, 2016). Significant care was taken when writing the methodology section to specify the exacts steps taken to sample artifacts and to analyze them. It will be easy for future researchers to replicate the current study. Additionally, the methodology selected for the current study was based on past study designs for content analyses, gap analyses, and for spatial data analyses (Eidsvik et al., 2017; Ghilani, 2017; Mechler, 2016; Zhang & Wildermuth, 2016). This step supported the credibility of the data collected. Following Cope's requirements for qualitative study credibility, records were kept on every URL addresses sampled, and a hard copy and digital copy of each sampled document was archived (Cope, 2014).

Another element of trustworthiness is transferability. Transferability means the findings can be "applied to other settings or groups" (Cope, 2014, p. 89). In the current study, a clear description of the population being studied was provided to make it easier for researchers and other interested groups to make decisions about the transferability of the findings from the current study. For example, the current study sampled disaster preparedness planning documents from organizations that serve the homeless during disasters. This included homeless shelters, local and state government agencies, religious organizations, and nonprofit organizations. Additionally, the samples were taken from across the United States, thereby gaining a comprehensive cross-section of organization's serving the homeless during disaster situations.

The final strategy used to promote the trustworthiness of the representation of the data collected in the current study was to carefully interpret the data so that conclusions did not go beyond what the data supported. Cope (2014) supports this strategy for creating authenticity, as it restricts researcher bias.

Results

RQ1: What are the best practices recommended by experts in managing the special needs of the homeless in regard to the emergency and disaster management processes: Mitigation, Preparedness, Response, and Recovery?

Table 2 - Dataset A

Strategic Theme	%	Strategic Theme	%	Strategic Theme	%
Evacuation plan	0.63	Recovery plan	0.38	Meet the special needs of the homeless	0.25
Shelter-in-Place Plan	0.63	Common Hazard Emergency Plans (i.e. Fire)	0.25	Long-term sheltering plan	0.13
Communication Plan	0.63	Hazard Specific Plans	0.25	Financial Impact Statement	0.13
Information Management Plan	0.63	Public Emergency Services & Contractors	0.25	Trauma-informed approach	0.13
Pre-event planning	0.63	Notification & Communications Systems	0.25	Re-Entry Plan for Post Evacuation	0.13
Emergency Response Team Contact List	0.5	Plan Distribution & Access Instructions	0.25	**75-100%**	
Revision History	0.5	Personal Preparedness Plans	0.25	50-74%	
Define Special Needs Populations	0.5	Health Status Plans	0.25	25-49%	
Outreach Teams	0.5	Business continuity plan	0.25	<25%	

Disaster Preparedness Planning for the Homeless

Collaboration Plan with Community Service Providers	0.5	Contingency plans	0.25
Mutual Aid Agreements	0.5	Risk Assessment	0.25
Chain of command/roles and responsibilities	0.5	Resource assessment	0.25
Lockdown Plan	0.38	Create disaster checklists	0.25
Medical Emergency Plan	0.38	Stakeholder analysis	0.25
Transportation Plans	0.38	Memorandum of Understanding	0.25
Staff Training	0.38	Form a disaster preparedness team	0.25
Identify where homeless congregate	0.38	Disaster preparedness plan	0.25
Response plan	0.38	Keep plans updated	0.25

Dataset A consisted of eight samples taken from organizations and individuals considered experts in the field of disaster preparedness. Samples were taken from general experts in disaster management, as well as from organization that specialized in disaster preparedness for vulnerable populations and for the homeless. The samples were templates, as opposed to completed disaster preparedness plans. The templates explained what organizations "should do" to prepare to serve the homeless during disasters, thereby establishing best practices.

Eight sources were sampled from organizations that are deemed to be experts in the field of emergency and disaster management and/or that are experts in disaster planning for homeless populations. A content analysis was conducted in which specific strategies for disaster management for service providers for the homeless. The data collected revealed three frequency groups. The first group contained disaster preparedness planning strategies that were found in less than 25% of the sources samples. This group included the strategies of having re-entry plans for post-evacuation situations, having long-term sheltering plans for the homeless post-disaster, creating a financial impact statement for critical incidents, and adopting a trauma-informed approach to disaster preparedness for homeless populations. The following are descriptions of the disaster preparedness activities found in Dataset A. The descriptions are based on the content found in the documents sampled and constructed by the researcher, as opposed to being a paraphrase of a description provided by the source.

Re-entry plans. A re-entry plan details how the homeless are to be moved back into the community following an evacuation order.

Long-term sheltering plans. A plan that permanently addresses high-risk zones in the community and providing long-term sheltering options post-disaster that are safe and out of the high-risk zones. This makes future disaster responses safer for first responders and rescue teams, as well as more efficient at locating where the homeless are congregating so they can be accessed for evacuations quicker.

Financial impact statement. A schedule that details short-term, medium-term, and long-term costs associated with disaster losses, rebuilding, and restoring the operation of homeless shelters and other services used by the homeless.

Trauma-informed approach. This strategy anticipates that a high percentage of the homeless have experienced traumas in the past and may need psychological and/or medical support and special handling.

The second frequency category of disaster preparedness strategies was made up of practices found in between 25 and 49% of the samples. Twenty-five themes were observed in this category. Themes in this group included: Lockdown plans, medical emergency plans, transportation plans, staff training, location mapping of where the homeless congregate in the community, response plans, recovery plans, common hazard emergency plans, hazard-specific plans, pubic emergency services and contractors contact information lists, notification and communication systems, plan distribution and access instructions, personal preparedness plans for staff, health status plans, business continuity plans, contingency plans, risk assessments, resource assessments, disaster checklists, stakeholder analyses, memorandums of understanding, the formation of disaster preparedness team, disaster preparedness plans, keeping disaster preparedness plans updated, and meeting the special needs of the homeless.

Lockdown plan. This document is used when the threat of violence is posed, and the organization needs to secure the building to protect staff and clients.

Medical emergency plan. This plan is used to respond to medical emergencies, such as heart attack, heat stroke, the presence of an infectious disease, a woman goes into labor, or someone has a serious injury. The plan defines what to do, where to find medical supplies, and who to contact.

Transportation plan. This plan describes how staff and clients are to be transported during a disaster response. It is executed during evacuations and when helping to get the homeless from their outside congregation areas to the homeless shelter and/or disaster shelter.

Staff training plan. This plan is used to define how staff is to be trained in the disaster preparedness and responses strategies. It includes training material, information about who will lead the training, who needs to be trained in each module, and how often the training should be completed.

Identify where homeless congregate. This assessment is important because the homeless do not have permanent residences, so it is difficult to know where to find them when an evacuation is ordered. However, the most efficient way to locate the homeless is to go where they normally congregate.

Response plan. This document clearly defines roles and responsibilities, resources, strategies, and management techniques for the disaster response effort. It is executed when a disaster strikes and continues until the threat is over and the situation is stabilized.

Recovery plan. This document is used to direct the recovery process. It identifies resources, people to contact for help, and objectives to achieve to repair damage and to return to normal operations.

Common hazard emergency plans. This plan is used to direct the response to common hazards, such as fires. It is a simple response plan that explains what to do, roles and responsibilities, evacuation routes, and other related information needed to respond to this group of hazards.

Hazard-specific plans. This plan is created for specific hazards, such as floods, hurricanes, extreme summer or winter weather, and tornadoes, that occur regularly in the community/region. They provide specific steps to take to secure the facility and protect the clients and staff during the hazard.

Public emergency services and contractors contact lists. This contact list is used to provide the contact of key public emergency services and contractors that are responsible for helping the homeless during and after a disaster.

Notification and communication systems. This system defines how information about a disaster is disseminated. The homeless do not have phones or reliable access to media, such as televisions and radios. Strategies need to be developed, therefore, to communicate with the homeless about the threat and what they need to do to get to a shelter.

Plan distribution and access instructions. This process is used to communicate with service providers for the homeless about disaster preparedness, response, and recovery strategies that are in place.

Personal preparedness plans. This set of plans are used to prepare employees of services providers to the homeless, so they are ready to manage the challenges of a disaster response and to ensure their disaster preparedness needs are met.

Health status plans. These plans are used to direct the assessment of the homeless during a disaster response. Since the homeless tend to have nontreated pre-existing medical and mental health issues, extra attention is needed to assess their health status so that their needs can be accommodated.

Business continuity plan. This plan is used to keep the organization's critical functions operational during and after a disaster.

Contingency plan. This plan provides the organization with alternative options for critical systems and resources, such as communication, power, and locations.

Risk assessment. This assessment identifies risk, quantifies their scope and severity of potential damage, and estimates their probability of occurring.

Resource assessment. This assessment inventories resources the organization currently has access to and also identifies resources held by other organizations that can be accessed during a disaster.

Create disaster checklists. Checklists are created for processes so that steps are not missed and to verify that a process was completed and by whom it was completed.

Stakeholder analysis. This analysis is used to identify stakeholders and to assess their interests, needs, contributions, and capabilities for a disaster response.

Memorandum of understanding. This memorandum establishes an understanding of what will be done and how during the disaster response. It is used to coordinate efforts between organizations.

Form a disaster preparedness team. The disaster preparedness team is responsible for conducting appropriate assessments, developing disaster preparedness plans and documents, implementing the plans, and training staff.

Disaster preparedness plan (comprehensive). The complete set of planning documents, checklists, and contact lists associated with an organization's disaster preparedness.

Keep plans updated. It is recommended that disaster preparedness and related plans be updated after each use and at least once a year.

Meet the special needs of the homeless. The homeless are a vulnerable population that have special needs. These needs include medical and mental health issues, lack of access to personal resources, and lack of adequate shelter and transportation. The homeless's special needs must be identified and met to prevent long-term problems from exposure to the trauma of a disaster.

The final frequency group included themes found in between 50 and 74% of the sampled sources. This group had 12 entries. They were: Evacuation plans, shelter-in-place plans, communication plans, information plans, pre-event planning, emergency response team contact list, revision history forms, defining special needs populations being served, having an outreach team, collaboration plans that involve community service providers, mutual aid agreements, and having a documented chain of command document that clearly defined roles and responsibilities.

Evacuation plan. A plan that defines how the organization and/or population of homeless will be evacuated to a disaster shelter. It includes a transportation plan.

Shelter-in-place plan. A plan that defines how to remain safe in the homeless shelter or facility if evacuation is not possible. It includes a resource needs list, strategies for securing the building, and instructions on how to set up a shelter inside the facility.

Communication plan. A plan that defines who communicates to whom, how, when, why, and what content.

Information management plan. A plan that includes a communication plan, but also directions on how to collect, manage, and respond to various pieces of information related to the disaster response and recovery effort. It also includes directions on what post-incident reports need to be created and who to distribute them to.

Pre-event planning. This strategy requires planning for a disaster to take place before a disaster takes place.

Emergency response team contact list. A list that lists the key emergency response team's contact information.

Revision history. A chart placed at the front or back of the disaster preparedness plan or other plans that documents when revisions were completed, what change was made, and who made them.

Define special needs populations. This strategy requires the organization to define special needs populations, such as the homeless and sub-populations within the homeless population so that special needs can be identified and planned for ahead of an incident.

Outreach teams. These teams go out into the community and connect with the homeless to identify their disaster preparedness needs, to distribute information about what to do when a disaster strikes, and to inform the homeless where evacuation shuttles will be located.

Collaboration plans with community service providers. This strategy encourages organizations serving the homeless to collaborate with the community disaster service providers, such as the local office of emergency and disaster management.

Mutual aid agreements. An agreement created between two organizations that indicates what resources will be shared during a disaster response.

Chain of command/roles and responsibilities chart. A chart that clearly shows the chain of command during a disaster. It is used to ensure succession is preplanned so that conflicts and disruptions command does not occur during a disaster response.

RQ2: What disaster preparedness steps are addressed by homeless shelters and other disaster service providers for the homeless?

A convenience sample was used to identify samples of existing disaster preparedness plans and activities for the homeless for Dataset B. Sampling involved searching the Internet for "disaster preparedness plans for the homeless," "homeless shelter disaster preparedness plan," and "homeless disaster preparedness." Dataset B consisted of 36 samples of disaster preparedness documents used by organizations that serve the homeless. The organizations served specific cities, counties, and states. The organizations served 17 states and Washington, D.C. The states included in the survey were Alabama, Alaska, Arizona, California, Colorado, Connecticut, Illinois, Indiana, Florida, Minnesota, Montana, New Mexico, New York, Oregon, Texas, Washington, Washington, D.C., and Wisconsin. Each document was scanned to determine what disaster preparedness activities it promoted, using the disaster preparedness list created for Dataset A as a base and adding new themes/activities as they were identified. Any theme identified from the list was marked with a value of one, and if a new theme was discovered in the current practices documents it was added to the list. After screening the 36 sampled documents, the only addition was mitigation efforts. A tally for each strategic theme was calculated and the percentage of prevalence in the 36 sampled documents was calculated. Table 2 summarizes the results for the Level A analysis.

Table 3 - Dataset B Level A Analysis

Strategic Theme	%	Strategic Theme	%
Collaboration Plans with Community Service Providers	69.4	Form a disaster preparedness team	8.3
Define Special Needs Populations	63.9	Common Hazard Emergency Plans (i.e. Fire)	5.6
Pre-event planning	41.7	Public Emergency Services & Contractors	5.6
Disaster preparedness plan	27.8	Notification & Communications Systems	5.6
Communication Plan	25	Risk Assessment	5.6
Hazard-Specific Plans	25	Memorandum of Understanding	5.6
Emergency Response Team Contact List	19.4	Keep plans updated	5.6
Response plan	19.4	Long-term sheltering plan	5.6
Meet the special needs of the homeless	19.4	Revision History	2.8
Chain of command/roles and responsibilities	16.7	Medical Emergency Plan	2.8
Shelter-in-Place Plan	13.9	Plan Distribution & Access Instructions	2.8
Outreach Teams	13.9	Health Status Plans	2.8
Resource assessment	13.9	Contingency plans	2.8
Staff Training	11.1	Re-Entry Plan for Post-Evacuation	2.8

Strategic Theme	%	Strategic Theme	%
Trauma-informed approach	11.1	Mitigation	2.8
Evacuation plan	8.3	Lockdown Plan	0
Information Management Plan	8.3	Personal Preparedness Plans	0
Mutual Aid Agreements	8.3	Business continuity plan	0
Transportation Plans	8.3	Create disaster checklists	0
Identify where homeless congregate	8.3	Stakeholder analysis	0

RQ3: What gaps exist between best practices recommended by FEMA and other experts and what homeless shelters and other disaster service providers for the homeless are currently doing regarding emergency and disaster preparedness planning?

The gaps in the strategic themes found between Dataset A and Dataset B were identified by examining where low frequencies in the themes were observed. Good compliance with best practices was defined as having more than 50% compliance among the current practice documents. The results showed that only two disaster preparedness practices from the best practices were found consistently in the current practices documents, creating collaboration plans to coordinate community service providers and defining special needs populations. The best practices that were not observed in any of the current practices documents were lockdown plans, personal preparedness plans, business continuity plans, disaster checklists and stakeholder analyses.

The second analysis used to answer research question 3 was data analysis Level B of the most commonly executed current practices. Since the compliance rate to best practices was so low, the three current practices that were completed most frequently were sampled to the Level B analysis. This level of analysis evaluated to what degree each practice was developed. A rating system of one to ten was used, with a score of one equating to being superficially developed and a score of ten equating to being fully developed. Table 3 summarizes the results.

Table 4 - Level B Analysis

Best Practice	Ave. Score
Collaboration Plans with Community Service Providers	3.5
Define Special Needs Populations	8.5
Pre-event planning	4.3

In response to the gaps observed, mitigation strategies taken from the literature review are aligned with each missing best practice. In Table 5, the missing best practice is listed, the second column provides the mitigation strategy, and column three identifies the source from the literature review where a description of the mitigation strategy can be found. Additionally, in Chapter Five, additional recommendations are made to further close the gaps identified.

Table 5 - Mitigation Strategies

Strategic Theme	Mitigation Strategy	Source
Disaster preparedness plan	Create a disaster preparedness plan	Haddow et al., 2013
Communication Plan	Use existing templates to create a communication plan or a crisis communication plan	FEMA, 2017; Rafferty-Semon et al., 2017
Hazard-Specific Plans	Create specific plans of action to prepare for and respond to specific types of hazards	Haddow et al., 2013
Emergency Response Team Contact List	Create contact lists for important people, partners, and service providers	U.S. Department of Labor, 2014
Response plan	Create a disaster response plan	FEMA (2014) "Emergency Response Plan;' FEMA (2017) National

		Preparedness; the HUD Exchange (2017)
Meet the special needs of the homeless	Train staff in psychological first aid	Hambrick et al., 2014
Chain of command/roles and responsibilities	Develop a chain of command with roles and responsibilities	Haddow et al., 2013
Shelter-in-Place Plan	Develop a shelter-in-place plan as a part of a disaster preparedness plan	Haddow et al., 2013
Outreach Teams	Develop, train, and utilize outreach teams to collect information about the homeless and to communicate with them about disaster preparedness and responses	Gin et al., 2015
Resource assessment	Create a disaster preparedness plan	Haddow et al., 2013
Staff Training	Train staff in how to implement all disaster preparedness plans	Haddow et al., 2013
Recovery plan	Create a recovery plan as a part of the complete	Haddow et al., 2013

	disaster preparedness plan	
Trauma-informed approach	Complete coursework/training on how to help victims of crisis or who have experienced a trauma	Aldunce, Beilin, Handmer, & Howden, 2014; Brassett & Vaughan-Williams, 2015; Plough et al., 2013
Evacuation plan	Create an evacuation plan as a part of a disaster preparedness plan with charts and maps	Haddow et al., 2013
Information Management Plan	Develop an Information Management Plan	van der Vegt, Essens, Wahlström, & George, 2015
Mutual Aid Agreements	Work with local organizations and service providers to create mutual aid agreements	Haddow et al., 2013
Transportation Plans	Develop a transportation plan for evacuations and moving the homeless to shelters	Haddow et al., 2013
Identify where homeless congregate	Create a map to identify common areas where the homeless congregate	U.S. Department of Housing and Urban Development, 2016

Form a disaster preparedness team	Recruit team members from the homeless shelter and from supporting service providers	Haddow et al., 2013
Common Hazard Emergency Plans (i.e. Fire)	Create a CHEP	Haddow et al., 2013
Public Emergency Services & Contractors	Create a contact list of important emergency services providers (First Responders)	Haddow et al., 2013
Notification & Communications Systems	Develop a communication plan	FEMA, 2017; Rafferty-Semon et al., 2017;
Risk Assessment	Conduct a risk assessment as part of creating a disaster preparedness plan	Haddow et al., 2013
Memorandum of Understanding	Write a MOU to preface the disaster preparedness plan	Haddow et al., 2013
Keep plans updated	Update all disaster preparedness plans at least annually	Haddow et al., 2013
Long-term sheltering plan	Develop long-term plans to address post-disaster relocation needs of the homeless	Gamboa-Maldonado, Marshak, Sinclair, Montgomery, & Dyjack, 2012; Miceli, Sotgiu, & Settanni, 2008

Revision History	Develop a simple chart to track changes made in the disaster preparedness plan	Haddow et al., 2013
Medical Emergency Plan	Create a MEP	Haddow et al., 2013
Plan Distribution & Access Instructions	Create a communication plan	FEMA, 2017; Rafferty-Semon et al., 2017;
Health Status Plans	Create HSPs for the homeless	Aldunce, Beilin, Handmer, & Howden, 2014; Brassett & Vaughan-Williams, 2015; Plough et al., 2013
Contingency plans	Develop contingency plans for critical functions and infrastructure	Boin, Stern, & Sundelius, 2016; Booth, 2015; Paton & Johnston, 2017
Re-Entry Plan for Post-Evacuation	Add a re-entry plan to the disaster preparedness plan	Haddow et al., 2013
Financial Impact Statement	Create a FIS to estimate the financial impact of disasters on the organization	Smith, 2007
Mitigation	Engage in mitigation planning and implementation throughout the disaster management cycle	Haddow et al., 2013; Paton & Johnston, 2017

Lockdown Plan	Create a lockdown plan for security threats	Haddow et al., 2013
Personal Preparedness Plans	Develop PPPs for employees	FEMA, 2017; Rafferty-Semon et al., 2017;
Business continuity plan	Develop a business continuity plan as a part of the disaster preparedness plan	Fuehrlein et al., 2014; Sahebjamnia, Torabi, & Mansouri, 2015
Create disaster checklists	Create checklists for what to do to prepare for, respond to, and recovery from disasters	Haddow et al., 2013
Stakeholder analysis	Create a stakeholder analysis using matrixes and narrative analyses	Berke, Smith. & Lyles, 2012; Sahebjamnia et al., 2015

RQ4: What vulnerabilities are created by the gaps in disaster preparedness planning for the homeless in the United States?

To answer research question four, data was collected from the FEMA "Disaster" (2018) page. This page offered a search engine for all disaster declarations found in the FEMA database. Disaster declaration data files were collected for the years 2012 through 2017. States were sampled based on where the organizations sampled for Dataset B were located. A total of 17 states and Washington, D.C. were sampled. The states sampled were: Alabama, Alaska, Arizona, California, Colorado, Connecticut, Illinois, Indiana, Florida, Minnesota, Montana, New Mexico, New York, Oregon, Texas, Washington, Washington, D.C., and Wisconsin. GIS-based maps were constructed to show what areas were impacted by disaster declarations and where homeless shelters were clustered. Disasters were sampled based on the availability of disaster impact maps produced by FEMA, which limited the disasters to only major events. The locations of the homeless shelters were identified using Google Earth. The maps were generated using JPEG files from Google Earth and ArcMap software. The maps produced were analyzed to assess if disasters were impacting areas where homeless tend to group.

Alabama

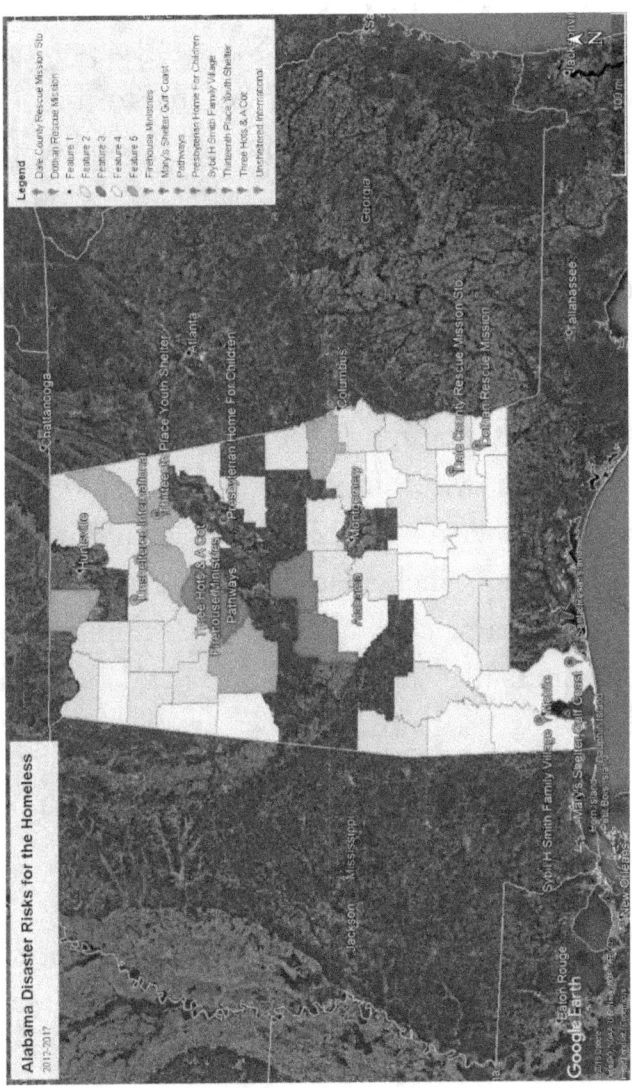

Figure 1 - Alabama Disaster Risks for the Homeless

The State of Alabama experienced five major disasters between the years of 2012 and 2017. They included Alabama Hurricane Nate (DR-4349) on November 16, 2017, Alabama Severe Storms, Tornadoes, Straight-Line Winds, and Flooding (DR-4251) on January 21, 2016, Alabama Severe Storms, Tornadoes, Straight-Line Winds, and Flooding (DR-4176), Alabama Hurricane Isaac (DR-4082) on May 2, 2014, and Alabama Severe Storms, Tornadoes, Straight-Line Winds, and Flooding (DR-4052). As Figure 1 illustrates, nearly the entire state of Alabama was impacted by one more major disasters or emergencies between 2012 and 2017. This impacted all the homeless shelters in the state, as well as the areas of Alabama covered under the sampled disaster preparedness plans, i.e. Montgomery, Alabama and Dale County, Alabama.

Alaska

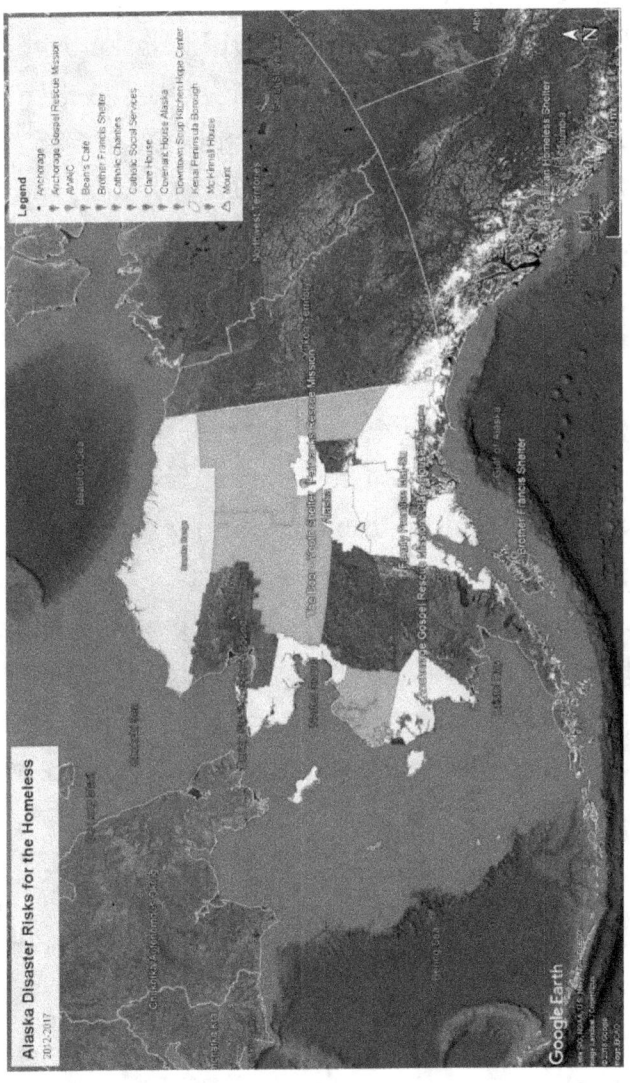

Figure 2 - Alaska Disaster Declarations and Homeless Shelter Locations

Between 2012 and 2017, FEMA issued eight disaster declarations. They were Alaska Severe Storm (DR-4351) on December 20, 2017, Alaska Severe Storm (DR-4257) on February 17, 2016, Alaska Severe Storm (DR-4244) on October 30, 2015, Alaska Severe Storms, Straight-Line Winds, and Flooding (DR-4162) on January 23, 2014), Alaska Flooding (DR-4161) on January 16, 2014, Alaska Flooding on June 25, 2013, and Alaska Severe Storm, Straight-Line Winds, Flooding, and Landslides (DR-4094) on November 2012). The distribution of the disasters showed high concentrations along the coast and where the majority of the population of the state lives, i.e. Anchorage and Juno. In Alaska, homeless shelters are limited to the major cities and are identified on the map where they are concentrated. Subsequently, the disaster preparedness plans sampled from Alaska came from organizations in Anchorage.

Arizona

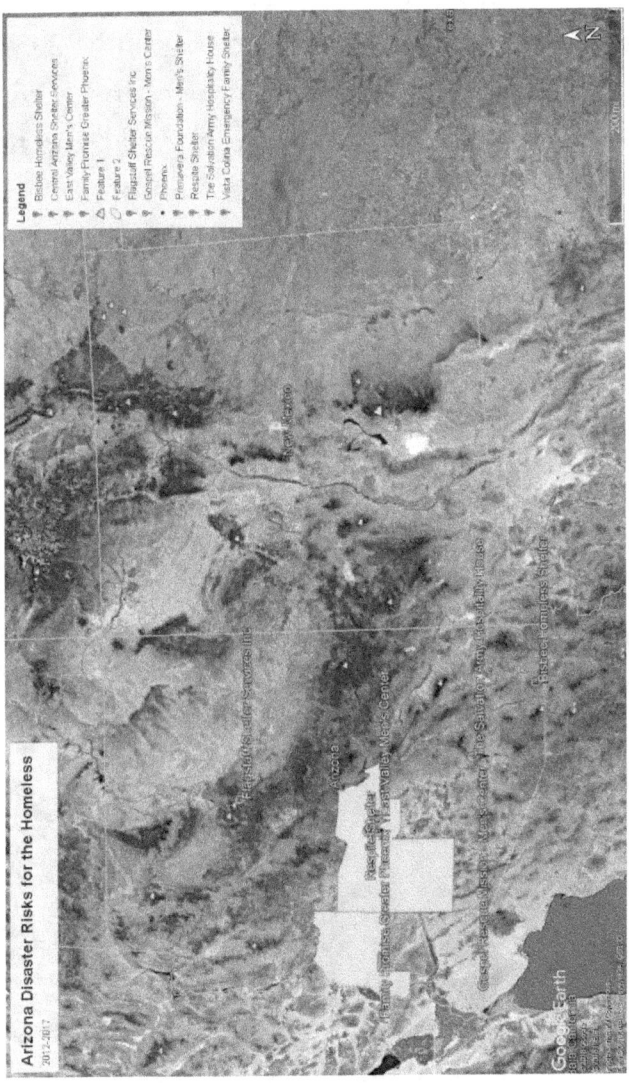

Figure 3 - Arizona Disaster Risks for the Homeless

FEMA recorded one major incident for the state of Arizona between 2012 and 2017. It was the Arizona Severe Storms and Flooding (DR-4203) on November 5, 2014. This incident overlapped where the state's homeless shelters are clustered, and the city covered by the disaster preparedness plan for the homeless, which was the city of Phoenix.

Disaster Preparedness Planning for the Homeless

California

Figure 4 - California Disaster Risks for the Homeless

The state of California experienced eleven major disasters between 2012 and 2017. They were California Wildfires (DR-4344) on October 10, 2017, Resighini Racheria Flooding (DR-4312) on May 2, 2017), California Severe Winter Storms, Flooding, Mudslides (DR-4308), California Severe Winter Storms, Flooding, and Mudslides (DR-4305) on March 16, 2018, Hoopa Valley Tribe Severe Winter Storm (DR-4302), California Severe Winter Storms, Flooding, and Mudslides (DR-4301) on February 14, 2017, California Valley Fire and Butte Fire (DR-4240) on September 22, 2015, Soboba Band of Luiseno Indians Severe Storms, Flooding, and Mudslides (DR-4206) on January 27, 2015, California Earthquake (DR-4193) on September 11, 2014, California Rim Fire (DR-4158) on December 13, 2013, and Karuk Tribe Wildfire (DR-4142) on August 29, 2013. Most of the state of California was impacted by disasters between 2012 and 2017. Every major city was located within a disaster zone. Subsequently, most of the homeless shelters in the state were also impacted by major disasters. Additionally, the areas covered by the disaster preparedness plans for the homeless also were found primarily in disaster-impacted areas. The areas where samples were taken included Los Angeles, San Diego

County, Alameda County, Tuolumne County, Stanislaus County, and La Palma.

Colorado

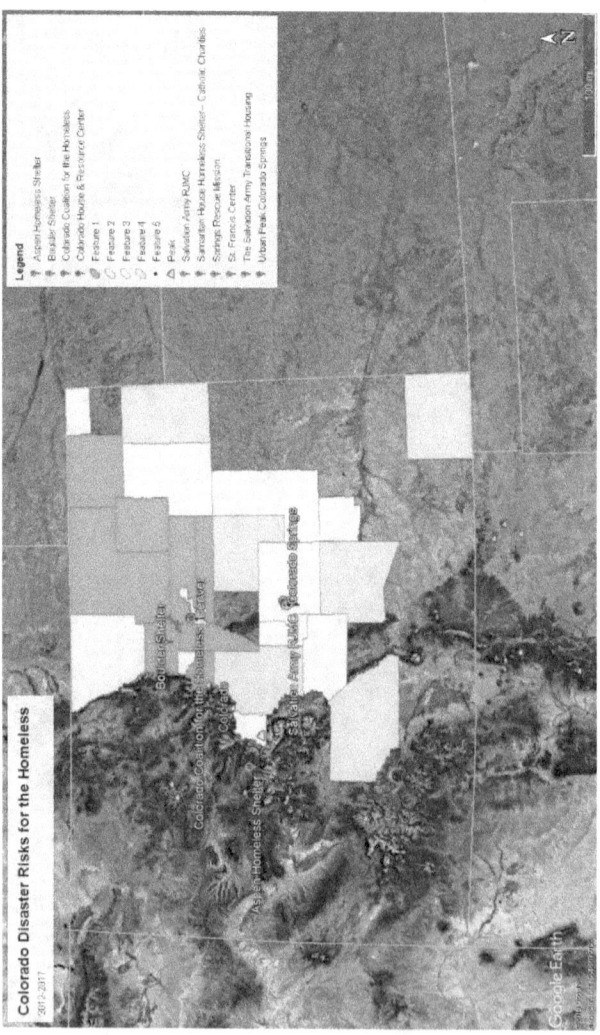

Figure 5 - Colorado Disaster Risks for the Homeless

Colorado experienced five major disasters between 2012 and 2017. They were Colorado Severe Storms, Tornadoes, Flooding, Landslides, and Mudslides (DR-4229) on July 19, 2015, Colorado Severe Storms, Flooding, Landslides, and Mudslides (DR-4145) on September 14, 2013, Colorado Royal Gorge Wildfire (DR-4133) on July 26, 2013, Colorado Black Forest Wildfire (DR-4134) on July 26, 2013, and Colorado High Park and Waldo Canyon Wildfires (DR-4067) on June 28, 2012. The majority of Colorado's homeless shelters are clustered in its largest cities, i.e. Denver and Colorado Springs, both of which were impacted by disasters between 2012 and 2017. Only the homeless shelters in Aspen were not impacted by disasters during the sampled period. Disaster preparedness plan samples for Colorado came from Denver, which was impacted by most of the major disasters in the sample period.

Connecticut

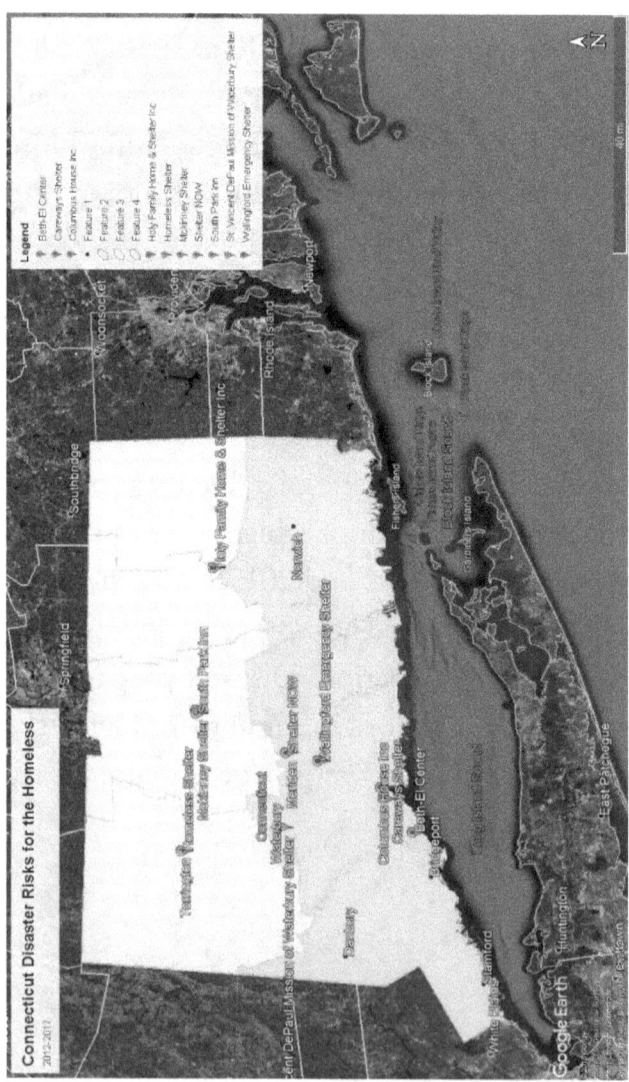

Figure 6 - Connecticut Disaster Risks for the Homeless

The state of Connecticut experienced three major disasters between 2012 and 2017. They were the Connecticut Severe Winter Storm and Snowstorm (DR-4213) declared on April 8, 2015, the Connecticut Severe Winter Storm and Snowstorm (DR-4106) declared on March 21, 2013, and the Connecticut Hurricane Sandy (DR-4087) declared on October 30, 2012. Since the entire state was impacted by one or more disasters during the sampled time frame, all of the state's homeless shelters were impacted, along with the organizations sampled for the study, which came from Stamford.

Florida

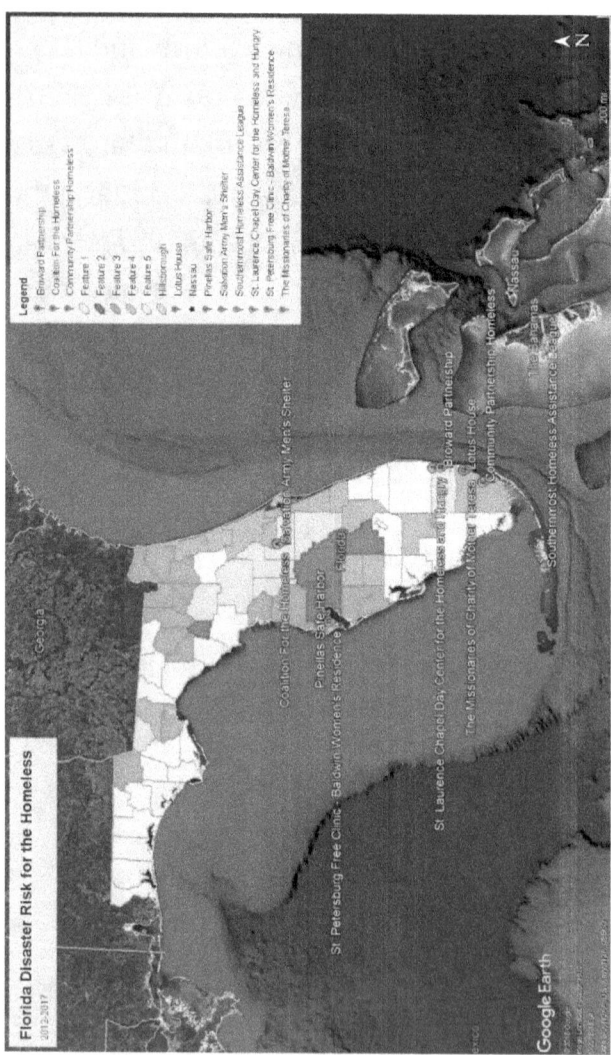

Figure 7 - Florida Disaster Risk for the Homeless

Florida experienced eight major disasters between 2012-2017. They were the Seminole Tribe of Florida Hurricane Irma – Seminole Tribe of Florida (DR_4341 declared on September 27, 2017, the Florida Hurricane Irma (DR-4337) declared on September 10, 2017, Florida Hurricane Matthew (DR-4283) declared on October 8, 2016, Florida Hurricane Hermine (DR-4280) declared on September 28, 2016, Florida Severe Storms, Tornadoes, Straight-Line Winds, and Flooding (DR-4177) declared on May 6, 2014, Florida Severe Storms and Flooding (DR-4138) declared on August 2, 2013, Florida Hurricane Isaac (DR-4084) declared on October 18, 2012, and Florida Tropical Storm Debby (DR-4068) declared on July 3, 2012. Disasters impacted the entire state of Florida, meaning that the state's entire homeless population was also impacted by disasters during the sample time frame. Additionally, every organization sampled for the study also was impacted. The sample organizations came from Pinellas County, Miami Dade County, and Orange Country.

Illinois

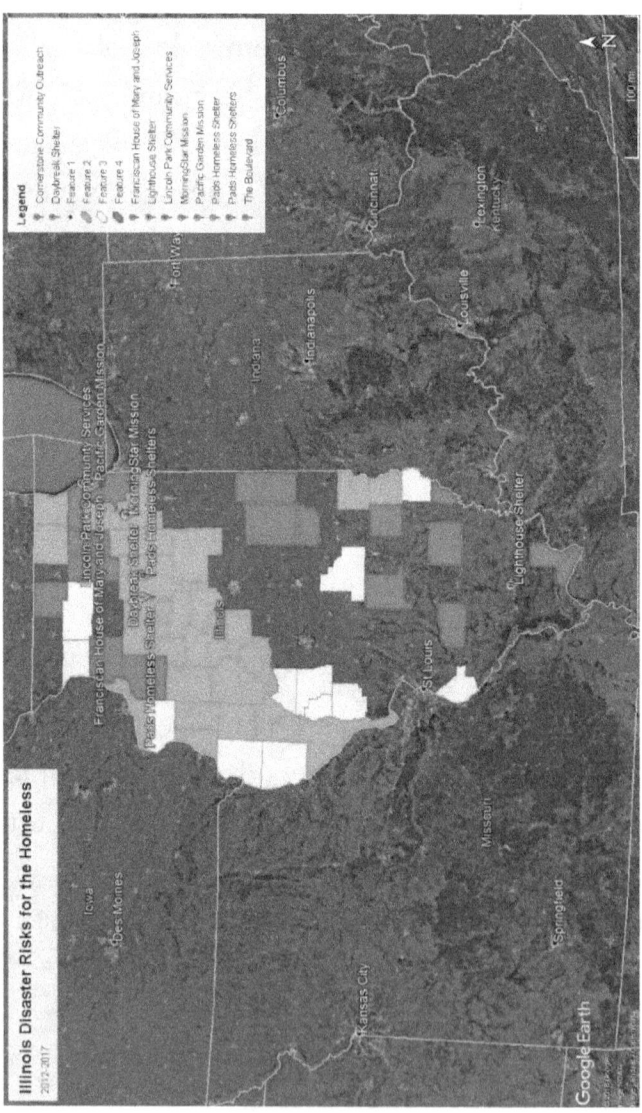

Figure 8 - Illinois Disaster Risks for the Homeless

The state of Illinois experienced two major disasters between 2012 and 2017. The first was the Illinois Severe Storms, Straight-Line Winds, and Tornadoes (DR-4157) declared on November 26, 2013, and the second was the Illinois Severe Storms, Straight-Line Winds, and Flooding (DR-4116) declared on May 10, 2013. The disaster path leads from Tornado Alley to the Great Lakes, putting the state's homeless shelters in the direct path of multiple natural hazards. The sample taken from this state came from Chicago, which is in the pathway of the major disasters experienced during the sample period.

Indiana

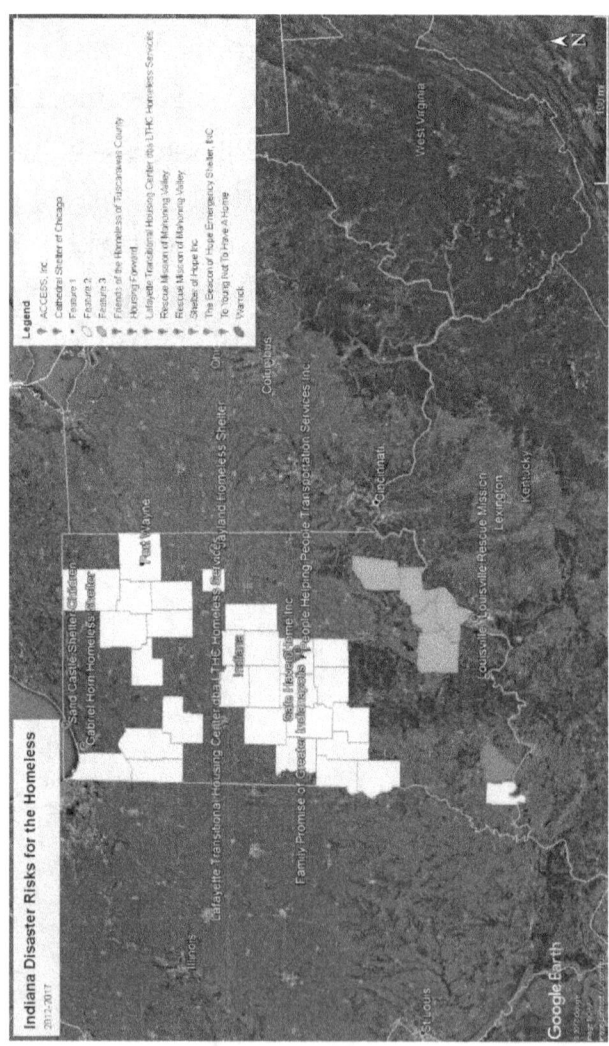

Figure 9 - Indiana Disaster Risks for the Homeless

FEMA declared two major disasters in Indiana between 2012 and 2017. The first was Indiana Severe Winter Storm and Snowstorm (DR-4173) declared on April 22, 2014, and the second was Indiana Severe Storms, Straight-Line Winds, and Tornadoes (DR-4058) declared on March 9, 2012. The homeless population was impacted by both of these disasters, especially in Indianapolis, which is where the disaster preparedness plan sample for the state derived.

Minnesota

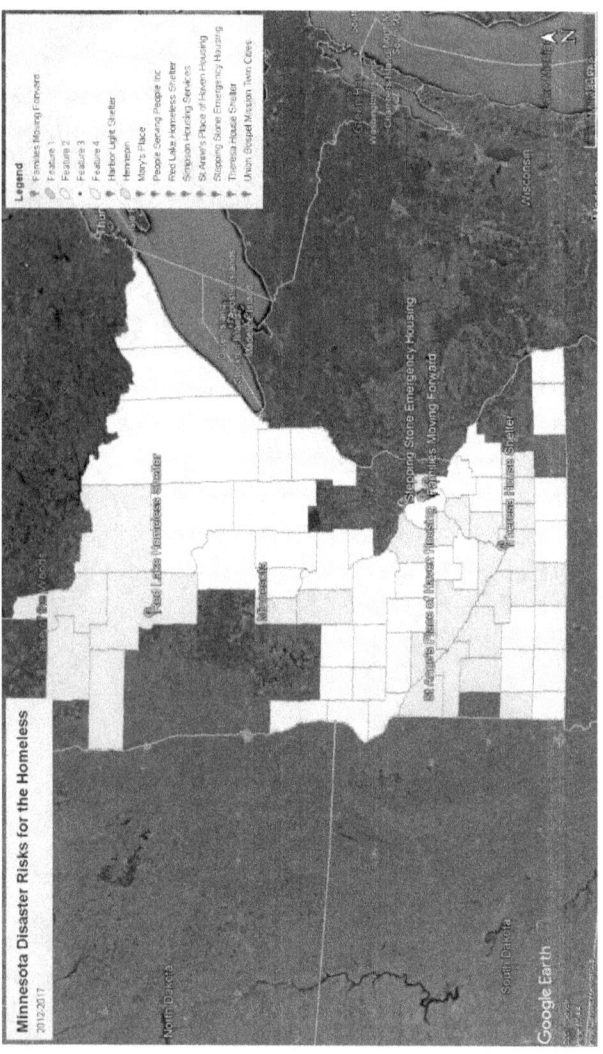

Figure 10 - Minnesota Disaster Risks for the Homeless

Five major disasters occurred in Minnesota between 2012 and 2017. They were Minnesota Severe Storms and Flooding (DR-4290) declared on November 2, 2016, Minnesota Severe Storms, Straight-Line Winds, Flooding, Landslides, and Mudslides (DR-4182) declared on July 21, 2014, Minnesota Severe Storms, Straight-Line Winds, and Flooding (DR-4131) declared on July 25, 2013, Minnesota Severe Winter Storm (DR-4113) declared on May 3, 2013, and Minnesota Severe Storms and Flooding (DR-4069) declared on July 6, 2012. The disasters that hit Minnesota impacted the areas where the state's homeless populations cluster, i.e. Minneapolis, which is where the disaster preparedness plan sample came from for this state.

Montana

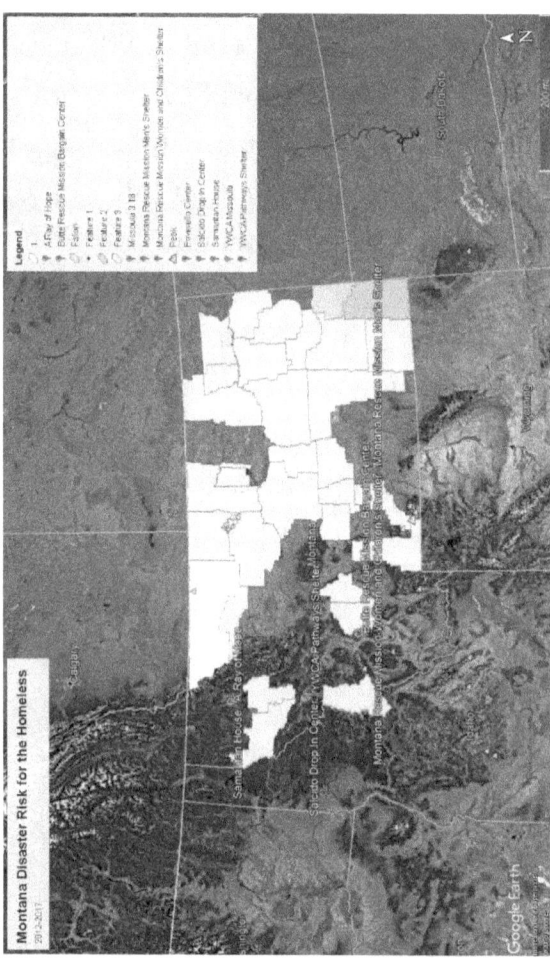

Figure 11 - Montana Disaster Risks for the Homeless

The state of Montana experienced six major disasters between 2012 and 2017. They were Montana Tornado (DR-4275) declared on August 3, 2016, Montana Severe Winter Storm and Straight-Line Winds (DR-4271) declared on May 24, 2016, Montana Severe Storms, Straight-Line Winds, and Flooding (DR-4198) declared on October 9, 2014, Montana Ice Jams and Flooding (DR-4172) declared on April 17, 2014, Montana Flooding (DR-4172) declared on July 10, 2013, and Montana Wildfires (DR-4074) declared on August 2, 2012. Most of the disasters that hit Montana impacted areas with low population densities. This protected the homeless population from being impacted by most disaster incidents. The disaster preparedness plan for the homeless sampled for this state came from Yellowstone County.

New Mexico

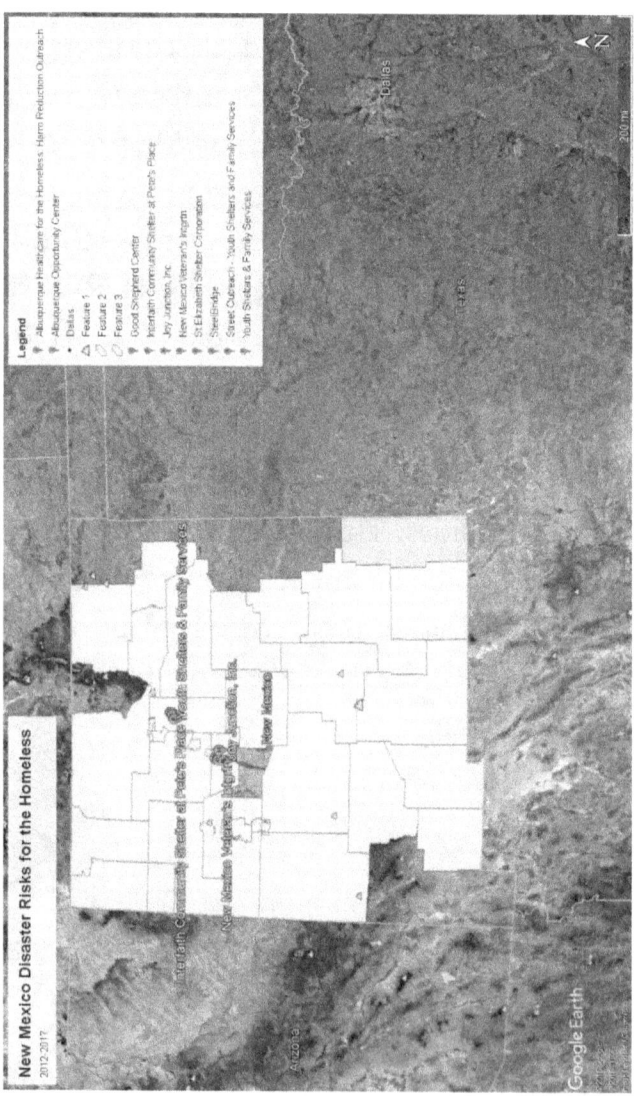

Figure 12- New Mexico Disaster Risks for the Homeless

New Mexico experienced eight major disasters between 2012 and 2017. They were the Pueblo of Acoma Severe Storms and Flooding (DR-4352) declared on December 20, 2017, New Mexico Severe Storms and Flooding (DR-4199) declared on October 29, 2014, New Mexico Severe Storms and Flooding (DR-4197) declared on October 6, 2014, New Mexico Severe Storms, Flooding, and Mudslides (DR-4152) declared on October 29, 2013, the Santa Clara Pueblo Severe Storms and Flooding (DR-4151) declared on October 24, 2013, the New Mexico Severe Storms and Flooding (Dr-4148) declared on September 30, 2013, Santa Clara Pueblo Severe Storms and Flooding (DR-4147) declared on September 27, 2013, and New Mexico Flooding (DR-4079) declared on August 24, 2012. The areas where the homeless cluster in New Mexico, Santa Fe and Albuquerque, were covered by the disaster preparedness plans sampled for this state and were impacted by disasters during the sample period.

New York

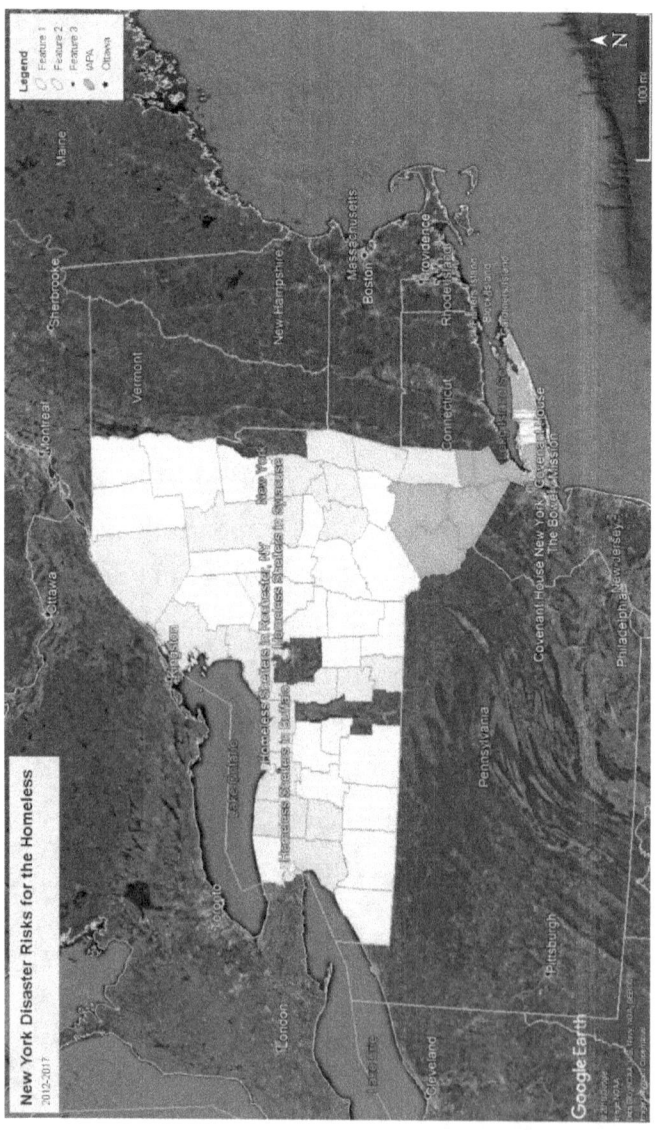

Figure 13 - New York Disaster Risks for the Homeless

The state of New York experienced seven disasters between 2012 and 2017. They were New York Flooding (DR-4348) declared on November 14, 2017, New York Severe Winter Storm and Snowstorm (DR-4322) declared on July 12, 2017, New York Severe Winter Storm, Snowstorm, and Flooding (DR-4204) declared on December 22, 2014, New York Severe Storms and Flooding (DR-4180) declared on July 8, 2014, New York Severe Storms and Flooding (DR-4129) declared on July 12, 2013, New York Severe Winter Storm and Snowstorm (DR-4111) declared on April 23, 2013, and New York Hurricane Sandy (DR-4085) declared on October 30, 2012. All major cities, including the sample city, New York City, were impacted by disasters, and subsequently, impacted the areas where the homeless cluster.

Oregon

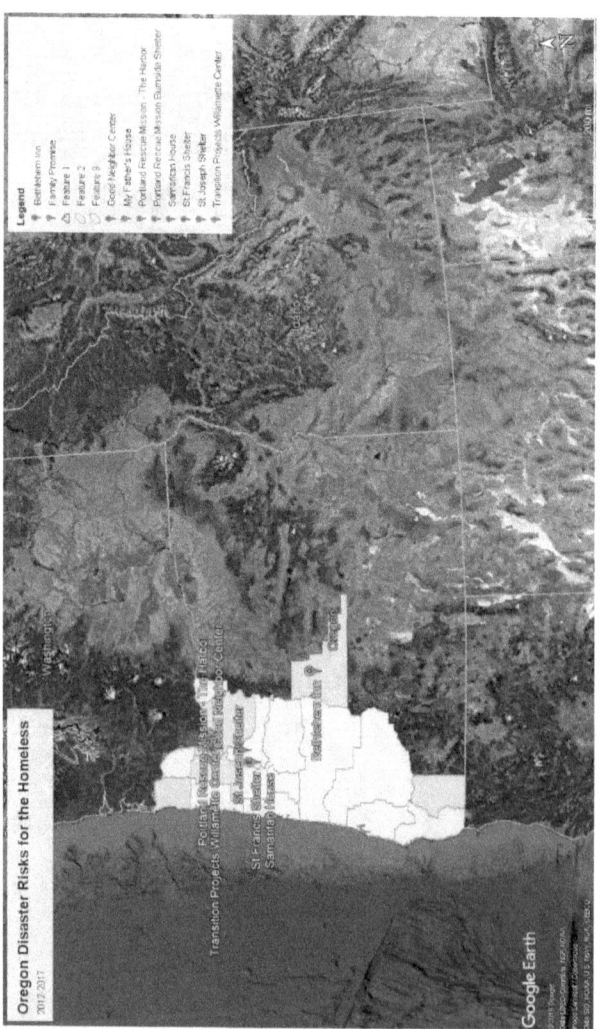

Figure 14 - Oregon Disaster Risks for the Homeless

Oregon experienced five major disasters between 2012 and 2017. They were Oregon Severe Winter Storms, Flooding, Landslides, and Mudslides (DR-4328) declared on August 8, 2017, Oregon Severe Winter Storm and Flooding (DR-4296) declared on January 25, 2017, Oregon Severe Winter Storms, Straight-Line Winds, Flooding, Landslides, and Mudslides (DR-4258) declared on February 17, 2016, Oregon Severe Winter Storm (DR-4169) declared on April 4, 2014, and Oregon Severe Winter Storm, Flooding, Landslides, and Mudslides (DR-4055) declared on March 2, 2012. The disasters impacted Oregon's most densely populated areas, Portland and its suburbs, which put the majority of the state's homeless at risk. The disaster preparedness plans for this state were sampled from organizations in the Portland area.

Texas

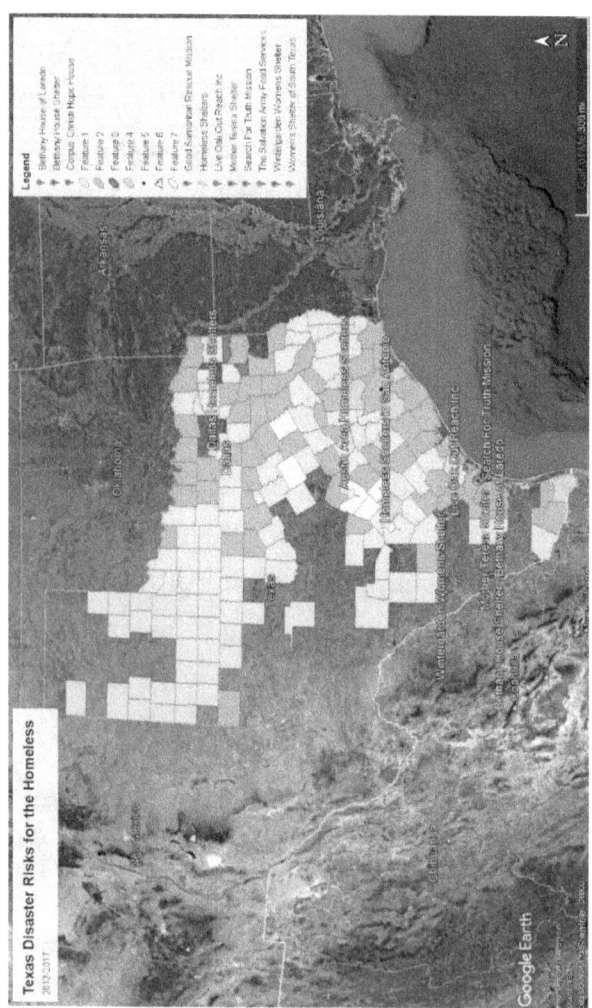

Figure 15 - Texas Disaster Risks for the Homeless

Texas experienced nine major disasters between 2012 and 2017. They were Texas Hurricane Harvey (DR-4332) declared on August 25, 2017, Texas Severe Storms and Flooding (DR-4272) declared on June 11, 2016, Texas Severe Storms and Flooding (DR-4269) declared on April 25, 2016, Texas Severe Storms, Tornadoes, and Flooding (DR-4266) declared on March 19, 2016, Texas Severe Winter Storms, Tornadoes, Straight-Line Winds, and Flooding (DR-4255) declared on February 9, 2016, Texas Severe Storms, Tornadoes, Straight-Line Winds, and Flooding (DR-4245) declared on November 25, 2015, Texas Severe Storms, Tornadoes, Straight-Line Winds, and Flooding (DR-4223) declared on May 29, 2015, Texas Explosion (DR-4136) declared on August 2, 2013. The areas where disasters struck impacted the most populated areas of the state. Organizations sampled for the study came from Houston, and Round Rock, Texas. When analyzed, the disasters clearly impacted where the homeless cluster in the state as well as impacted the organizations sampled for analysis.

Washington

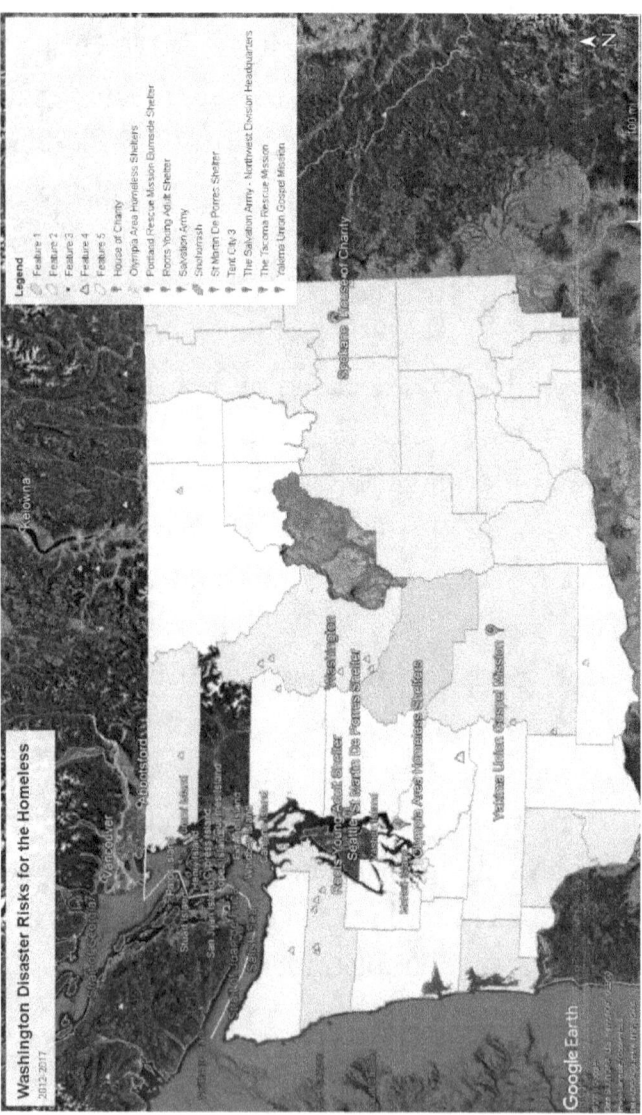

Figure 16 - Washington Disaster Risks for the Homeless

The state of Washington experienced nine major disasters. They were Washington Severe Winter Storms, Flooding, Landslides, and Mudslides (DR-4309), Washington Severe Winter Storm, Straight-Line Winds, Flooding, Landslides, Mudslides, and a Tornado (DR-4253) declared on February 2, 2016, Washington Severe Storms, Straight-Line Winds, Flooding, Landslides, and Mudslides (DR-4249) declared on January 15, 2016, Washington Wildfires and Mudslides (DR-4243) declared on October 20, 2015, Washington Severe Windstorm (DR-4242) declared on October 15, 2015, Washington Wildfires (DR-4188) declared on August 11, 2014, Washington Flooding and Mudslides (DR-4168) declared on April 2, 2014, Washington Severe Storm, Straight-Line Winds, and Flooding (DR-4083) declared on September 25, 2012, and Washington Severe Winter Storm, Flooding, Landslides, and Mudslides (DR-4056) declared on March 5, 2012. Every major city in Washington was impacted by one or more disasters during the sampled time frame. Subsequently, the areas where homeless tend to cluster, such as Seattle and Tacoma, were also impacted. The organizations sampled for the study were Seattle and Tacoma, Washington.

Washington, D.C.

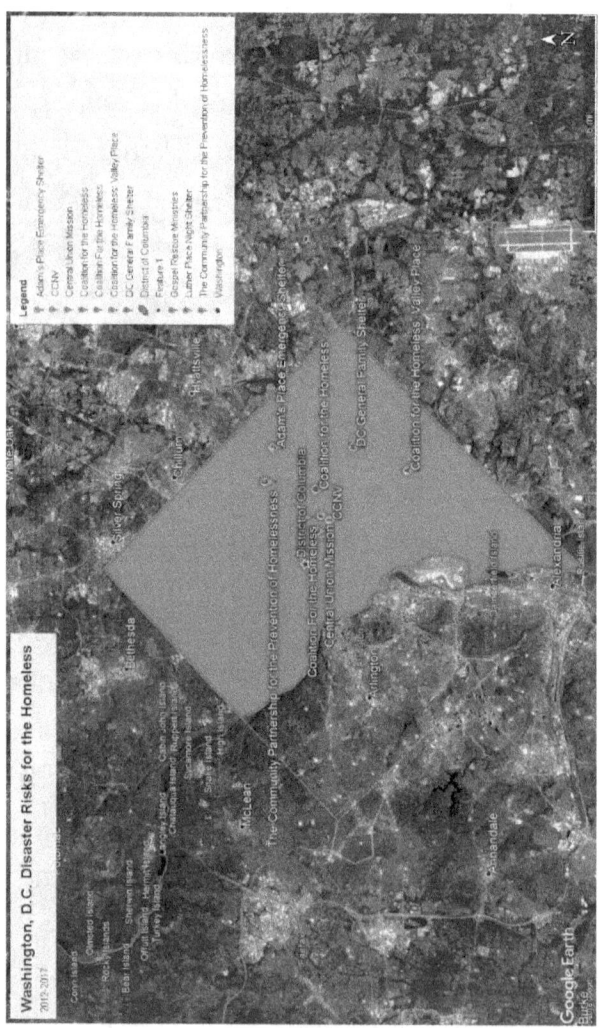

Figure 17 - Washington, D.C. Disaster Risks for the Homeless

Washington, D.C. experienced three major disasters between 2012 and 2017. They were District of Columbia (DC) Snowstorm (DR-4260) declared on March 4, 2016, District of Columbia (DC) Hurricane Sandy (DR-4096) declared on December 5, 2012, and District of Columbia (DC) Severe Storms (DR-4073) declared on July 31, 2012. The entire homeless population in Washington, D.C. was impacted by disasters during the sample period. One sample was collected for this city, and it covered the Washington, D.C. metropolitan area.

Wisconsin

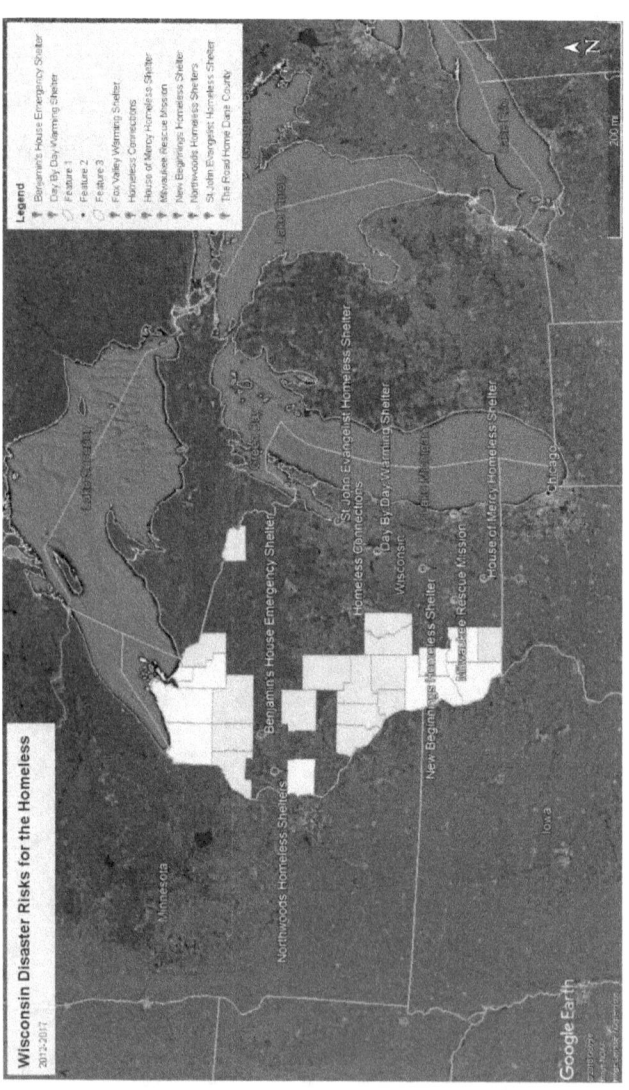

Figure 18 - Wisconsin Disaster Risks for the Homeless

The state of Wisconsin experienced five major disasters between 2012 and 2017. They included Wisconsin Severe Storms, Straight-Line Winds, Flooding, Landslides, and Mud (DR-4343) declared on October 7, 2017, Wisconsin Severe Storms, Flooding, and Mudslides (DR-4288) declared on October 20, 2016, Wisconsin Severe Storms and Flooding (DR-4276) declared on August 9, 2016), Wisconsin Severe Storms, Flooding, and Mudslides (DR-4141) declared on August 8, 2013, and Wisconsin Severe Storms and Flooding (DR-4076) declared on August 2, 2012. The disaster preparedness plan sample was taken from Waunakee, Wisconsin, which is located north of Madison, where the population in the state is dense.

Evaluation of the Findings

RQ1: What are the best practices recommended by experts in managing the special needs of the homeless in regard to the emergency and disaster management processes: Mitigation, Preparedness, Response, and Recovery?

When analyzing Dataset A, forty-one strategic themes were identified. Originally, to be considered a best practice, the threshold for selection was set at being present in 75% or more of the sources sampled. However, none of the strategic themes were present in 75% or more of the sources sampled. This shows that there is a great level of variability in what disaster strategies are recommended to organizations that provide disaster planning, response, and recovery services for the homeless.

The results from the analysis of best practices were inconsistent with the information presented in the literature review. The findings from the current study aligned with the expectations created by the literature review in that the information in the literature review indicated that disaster preparedness was a standardized process, but that it was also scalable (Haddow et al., 2013). This means that, depending on the needs of the people or organization engaging in disaster preparedness, the procedures and strategies implemented would vary (Donahue et al., 2017; Haddow et al., 2013). However, where the findings deviated from the findings in the literature was in regard to the standardization of the disaster preparedness process. Haddow et al. (2013) established that the disaster preparedness process needed to plan for the total disaster management cycle, including mitigation, preparedness, response, and recovery. The findings from the current study, however, showed that different experts on disaster preparedness promoted different scopes of preparedness activities for organizations serving the homeless. This difference is explained by literature findings that showed organizations not mandated to engage in disaster preparedness activities prepare at-will (Lowe et al., 2015; Sommer et al., 2016). Subsequently, some organizations focus on business continuity planning, while others do not engage in any preparedness activities (Cutter et al., 2013; Fuehrlein et al., 2014; Sahebjamnia et al., 2015).

RQ2: What disaster preparedness steps are addressed by homeless shelters and other disaster service providers for the homeless?

The analysis of Dataset B also reinforced the variability in what organizations completed in terms of disaster preparedness activities. The observations made of the data collected were that most of the practices identified in Dataset A were also found in Dataset B, but compliance rates were very low per disaster preparedness activity. For example, the highest compliance rate for a single disaster preparedness activity among the sampled organizations was 69.4% and only three activities were found in 40% or more of the samples. The conclusion drawn about this observation is that organizations responsible for disaster preparedness for the homeless are not engaging fully in the disaster preparedness process. For example, most of the artifacts sampled only defined the homeless as a special needs or vulnerable population and that a specific organization was responsible for addressing their needs during a disaster. Since the disaster preparedness documents were not available only from the organizations assigned responsibility for the homeless during a disaster, it is not possible at this time to conclude that organizations are not planning for the disaster needs of the homeless. However, what can be concluded is that homeless shelters are not preparing for disaster. This point is backed up by the data collected in the current study, as well as by the literature reviewed earlier. For example, Persson and Povitkina (2017) reported that political barriers and inefficiencies make disaster preparedness for the homeless problematic. This was seen in Dataset B where planning activities failed to assign responsibility for preparing the homeless or assigned responsibility without implementing accountability measures. Walters and Gaillard (2014) confirmed that marginalized populations, such as the homeless, are underserved by government and organization-level disaster preparedness, especially in regard to recovery and mitigation activities. Dataset B also illustrated this problem, in that only 5.6% of the documents sampled included long-term disaster planning activities or concern. Additionally, in some of the documents, it was specifically stated that disaster service for the homeless was restricted to disaster response only, and that no long-term rehousing efforts would be made. It was important to note this difference because long-term recovery assistance for rehousing non-homeless populations was offered and stressed as being important to the recovery of the community. This shows that communities are willing to invest in the recovery of previously housed residents but unwilling to invest in housing for the previously homeless residents. Finally, Fogel (2016) provided direct evidence that the people who are assigned responsibility for disaster preparedness activities for the homeless are not meeting that responsibility. In this case study, Fogel (2016) revealed that the homeless were not provided with disaster assistance, were often segregated from the mainstream population in disaster shelters, and otherwise mistreated and neglected during the official disaster response effort. The implication of these observations is that documenting roles and responsibilities for the homeless in official disaster preparedness plans is insufficient if accountability for meeting those responsibilities is not established and enforced.

***RQ3:** What gaps exist between best practices recommended by FEMA and other experts and what homeless shelters and other disaster service providers for the homeless are currently doing regarding emergency and disaster preparedness planning?*

The gap analysis showed that only three activities identified in the best practices content analysis were found in 50% or more of the sampled documents. Based on the literature reviewed, this can be explained by the scalability quality of disaster preparedness (Haddow et al., 2013). However, it also suggests that organizations responsible for disaster preparedness for the homeless are not engaging effectively in preparedness activities. This point is reinforced by the results produced by the Level B data analysis of Dataset B. The results from this analysis showed that the level of development of the three best practices identified in Dataset A and B was generally very low. For example, Pre-Event Planning activities had an average development score of 4.3 out of 10 and the Collaboration with Community Service Providers had an average development score of 3.5 out of 10. These low development scores indicate that even when disaster preparedness activities are completed, they are completed superficially. For example, only listing roles and responsibilities or only defining the homeless population. The conclusion drawn is that not only are there gaps in compliance with best practices, but that when best practices are executed, they are not executed effectively.

    The literature backs up the conclusion that organizations serving the homeless during disasters are not doing enough to prepare for disasters. It does this, first, by explaining why preparedness deficits exist. For example, Adams et al. (2013) reported ineffective disaster preparedness takes place because most companies lack talent that is trained in disaster management techniques. Additionally, Persson and Povitkina (2017) showed in their study that ineffective preparedness occurs when political barriers are created in the emergency and disaster management system. This was seen in the data collected in Dataset B, as effective planning was limited by political interest and by the reluctance of any agency or organization to take responsibility for disaster preparedness responsibilities for the homeless.

    Secondly, the literature supports the conclusion that organizations are underserving the homeless during disasters because of ineffective preparedness efforts by describing examples of the consequences of ineffective disaster preparedness. For example, the study by Fogel (2017), showed that the homeless were neglected during response effort, resulting in high rates of mortality and long-term health consequences. The neglect documented included failing to evacuate the homeless, failing to provide disaster response services to the homeless, and ill-treatment of the homeless at disaster shelters (Fogel, 2017). These failures demonstrate that ineffective disaster preparedness for the homeless has detrimental impacts on homeless individuals.

RQ4: *What vulnerabilities are created by the gaps in disaster preparedness planning for the homeless in the United States?*

The spatial data analysis revealed that in most of the states sampled, there was a significant overlap in where major disasters impacted human populations and where the homeless tend to cluster. Additionally, since most of the major disasters documented related to severe weather patterns, such as extreme heat or extreme cold, the need for the homeless to be able to access shelters that are functional is also extreme. Based on the conclusions drawn from research questions one, two, and three, homeless shelters are not adequately prepared for common or extraordinary disasters, and no one else in the community is preparing to offer homeless assistance. Subsequently, the conclusion drawn for research question four is that the gaps observed about disaster preparedness planning for the homeless in the United States is making them more vulnerable to acute traumas and long-term adverse psychological and physical problems. This conclusion is supported by the literature reviewed. For example, Gin et al. (2016) reported that following a disaster, the homeless were more likely to sustain life-threatening injuries and illnesses than the general public and are more likely to experience long-term consequences of surviving a disaster because the community fails to plan for long-term post-disaster assistance for this sub-population. Similarly, the study by Moyniham (2012) showed that inadequate disaster preparedness for the homeless reduced the homeless' ability to self-prepare for disasters. For example, communication barriers prevented the homeless from being warned about impending disasters, such as floods, hurricanes, and extreme weather.

Summary

The data from the current study revealed a picture of disaster preparedness for the homeless in the United States. First, the data revealed that there is a significant level of variability in what is considered to be a best practice for disaster preparedness, both in general and specifically for organizations serving the homeless. The practices found in 50% or more of the expert samples were evacuation plans, shelter-in-place plans, communication plans, information management plans, pre-event planning, emergency response team contact lists, revision histories for disaster preparedness plans, definitions for special needs populations, outreach teams, collaboration plans with community service providers, mutual aid agreements, and chain of command/roles and responsibilities charts. Second, the data showed that the scalability of the main disaster preparedness model allowed for organizations serving the homeless to choose what activities to engage in and which ones to omit. The results appear to be that most organizations serving the homeless during disasters are either not completing any disaster preparedness activities or are only superficially completing disaster preparedness activities. The three disaster preparedness activities completed by the most by the sampled organizations were collaboration plans with community service providers, define special needs populations, and engage in pre-event planning. These activities were found in more than 40% of the sampled documents. Third, the Level B analysis revealed that not only are the sampled organizations not completing the best practices as identified in the findings from Dataset A, but they are also only superficially completing the disaster preparedness activities they choose to complete. This was seen in the low average scores for best practice compliance. Finally, the study showed that the gaps in compliance with best practices for disaster preparedness by organizations serving the homeless are creating significant vulnerabilities for acute and long-term problems for the homeless. This conclusion is based on the observation that major disasters impacting states are impacting the areas where homeless tend to cluster and the findings that show organizations serving the homeless during disasters are not complying with best practices for disaster preparedness, and when they do complete an activity, it is not developed beyond transferring the responsibility to serve the homeless to another organization.

CHAPTER FIVE: IMPLICATIONS, RECOMMENDATIONS, & CONCLUSIONS

The problem addressed by the current study was the failure to plan adequately for the special disaster response and recovery needs of the homeless, a vulnerable population, resulted in devastating consequences. The purpose of the study was to define disaster preparedness gaps between what best practices prescribed for disaster preparedness, as identified by FEMA and emergency and disaster management experts, and what strategies organizations serving the homeless during disasters completed. A multi-stage qualitative analysis was conducted that included a content analysis of best practices and current practices, a gap analysis that compared best practices to current practices, and a spatial data analysis of disaster risks for the homeless.

The results from the study presented that a considerable amount of variability existed in defining disaster preparedness best practices and in what organizations serving the homeless did to prepare for disasters. Furthermore, the results showed that ineffective and inadequate disaster preparedness for the homeless was extremely neglectful and hazardous because the homeless tend to cluster in areas of states where major disasters are most likely to impact. Subsequently, not only are the homeless more vulnerable to the immediate impacts of a disaster, but also more vulnerable to long-term mental and physical health problems as well.

While the current study utilized trustworthy processes to collect and analyze data, the study was limited because of the lack of access to some organization's disaster preparedness planning documents. For example, in the documents sampled, often the only indicator of current planning for the homeless were lists of what organizations were responsible for disaster preparedness for the homeless. When those organization's websites were accessed, no documents were publicly available. Future research, therefore, needs to focus on directly studying the organizations officially assigned responsibility for prepared to serve the homeless during disasters.

In the following chapter, the implications of the current study are discussed. The discussions are organized by research questions and findings from the current study are connected to the findings of the studies sampled in the literature review. Finally, recommendations for practice and future research are provided to bring the study to a productive conclusion.

Implications

RQ1: *What are the best practices recommended by experts in managing the special needs of the homeless in regard to the emergency and disaster management processes: Mitigation, Preparedness, Response, and Recovery?*

The findings from the content analysis of Dataset A revealed that what is considered a best practice varies depending on what level of society is involved. For example, at the government level, best practices follow FEMA standards and disaster preparedness theory. At this level, best practices include "a continuous cycle of planning, organizing, training, equipping, exercising, evaluating, and taking corrective action in an effort to ensure effective coordination during incident response" (DHS, 2017, para. 1). However, the execution of these steps is highly variable between organizations and experts providing guidance. At the organization level, best practices are even more variable, with no clear best practice pattern. This is seen in the lack of any best practice being observed in more than 62.5% of the documents sampled in Dataset A. The level of variability observed can be explained by two factors. First, disaster preparedness is an emerging discipline that is still evolving (Llewellyn et al., 2016). This means that experts are still defining and debating about what should be considered a best practice. Second, the FEMA model of emergency and disaster management is defined as scalable (Haddow et al., 2013). This means that each organization and/or individual selects the disaster preparedness activities that are perceived as important and necessary for them. This naturally leads to a great variability in the variety of disaster preparedness activities developed and implemented.

RQ2: What disaster preparedness steps are addressed by homeless shelters and other disaster service providers for the homeless?

Dataset B described the disaster preparedness steps completed by homeless shelters and other disaster services providers for the homeless. The findings revealed 37 different activities, including one activity not observed in Dataset A. They were, in order of prevalence, collaboration plans with community services providers, define special needs populations, pre-event planning, disaster preparedness plan, communication plan, hazard-specific plans, emergency response team contact list, response plan, meet the special needs of the homeless, chain of command/roles and responsibilities list, shelter-in-place plan, outreach teams, resource assessment, staff training, recovery plan, trauma-informed approach, evacuation plan, information management plan, mutual aid agreement, transportation plan, identify where homeless congregate, form a disaster preparedness team, common hazard emergency plans, public emergency services and contractors, notification and communications systems, risk assessment, memorandum of understanding, keep plans updated, long-term sheltering plan, revision history, medical emergency plan, plan distribution and access instructions, health status plans, contingency plans, re-entry plan for post-evacuation, financial impact statement, mitigation, lockdown plan, personal preparedness plans, business continuity plan, create disaster checklists, and stakeholder analysis. As seen in the best practice (Dataset A), a high level of variability in disaster preparedness practices was seen in current practices (Dataset B). None of the activities listed were found in greater than 69.4% of the sampled documents, and most of the activities listed were found in less than 30% of the samples. The implication is that there is no standard in place for what disaster preparedness tasks organizations serving the homeless need to complete. This is not surprising because mandates and professional expectations for organization-level disaster preparedness are greatly missing. Only high-risk organizations, such as hospitals, utility companies, and organizations handling hazardous materials are required to have disaster preparedness plans in place (Veeneema, Losinski, & Hilmi, 2016). All other organizations are given individual discretion to choose what disaster preparedness activities to complete.

RQ3: *What gaps exist between best practices recommended by FEMA and other experts and what homeless shelters and other disaster service providers for the homeless are currently doing regarding emergency and disaster preparedness planning?*

The gap analysis revealed that most of the disaster preparedness activities identified in Dataset A (Best Practices) were observed in at least one current practice document. The only tasks not found in any of the current disaster preparedness documents were lockdown plans, personal preparedness plans, business continuity plans, disaster checklists, and stakeholder analyses. Since most of these activities align with business practices, it is possible that they are documented in private files not made available to the public. The remaining disaster preparedness planning tasks were observed in the sampled documents, but most organizations did not engage in more than one or two activities. Subsequently, all but three activities were found in less than 30% of the samples. The three activities found in more than 30% of the samples were collaboration plans (69.4%), defining special needs populations (63.9%), and pre-event planning (41.7%). These findings suggest that disaster preparedness among organizations responsible for the homeless during a disaster is incomplete or neglected. Additionally, when the three most common current practices were analyzed at the B Level, the results showed that only one out of the three activities were developed fully. The tasked developed fully was defining special needs populations. The only reason this one scored high in the Level B analysis was that it was a simple process. The implication of these findings is that, not only are organizations responsible for homeless disaster preparedness not completing the full spectrum of best practices, but the activities they are completing are not fully developed. This too was not surprising, as a common complaint cited in the literature was a lack of disaster planning and preparedness for the homeless (Fogel, 2016; Gin et al., 2016; Nicolay et al., 2016; Persson & Povitknia, 2017; Settembrino, 2017; Sundareswaran et al., 2015; Vickery, 2015; Walters & Gaillard, 2014). Additionally, the literature established that this deficit in disaster preparedness is not limited to organizations serving the homeless. It is also common among organizations serving other vulnerable populations, such as the elderly, non-English speakers, and the disabled (Agboola et al., 2015; Asioda et al., 2015; Lane & McGrady, 2016; Tosh eta l., 2014; U.S. Department of Housing and Urban Development, 2016; Van DeVaneter et al., 2017; Walsh et al., 2015). This indicates a systemic wide gap at the organization level for disaster preparedness, especially among organizations serving vulnerable populations.

When evaluated, the list of gaps created clear needs for mitigation efforts. In response to these needs, mitigation strategies from the literature review were aligned with each gap listed. When trends in the mitigation efforts were evaluated the result was that there was a need for organizations serving the disaster preparedness and response needs of the homeless to complete a full disaster preparedness plan. However, as established in the analysis of best practices, there is no consensus for what non-mandated organizations should do to prepare for disasters. Subsequently, the need that remains is for a disaster preparedness plan to be developed specifically for organizations serving the homeless.

RQ4: *What vulnerabilities are created by the gaps in disaster preparedness planning for the homeless in the United States?*

The spatial data analysis revealed that there is significant overlap between where the homeless cluster and where major disasters cluster in states. This is not an unexpected outcome. Major cities tend to lie in areas that are high-risk for disasters, such as near bodies of water (rivers, lakes, and the ocean), and in areas that are prone to regular natural disasters (floods, tornadoes, hurricanes, and earthquakes). Additionally, many of the causes of major disaster declarations have near-statewide impacts, leaving no safe place for the homeless to go to wait out the incident. The implication is that it is critical for organizations serving the homeless to engage in disaster preparedness planning because they are highly likely to be impacted by a disaster multiple times a year. The case studies reviewed in the literature review highlighted the consequences of failing to plan for the disaster response needs of the homeless, including the abandonment of homeless during disasters, the death of homeless due to disaster hazards and secondary traumas, and the inability to support the special needs of the homeless during and after a disaster (Fogel, 2016; Persson & Povitkina, 2017; Walters & Gaillard, 2014). This means that failure to plan for the disaster preparedness needs of the homeless creates short-term and long-term vulnerabilities to injuries, illness, and psychological disorders.

Recommendations for Practice

The theoretical framework for the current study has two foci, resilience building and contingency planning. The findings from the study indicate that neither is being accomplished with any degree of consistency among organizations serving the homeless during disasters. Subsequently, three recommendations for practice are suggested.

Standardize the process. The first recommendation is to standardize the disaster preparedness process for organizations serving the homeless during a disaster. The literature links disaster preparedness with resilience, meaning that organizations that fully engage in disaster preparedness activities will be more resilient to the effects of disasters than organizations who fail to prepare or who underprepared for disasters (Cavallo & Ireland, 2014). Based on the data collected, however, there is inconsistency in what disaster preparedness activities organizations complete and in what degree of development takes place. Standardization of the disaster preparedness process, therefore, will promote each organization complete the minimum amount of preparedness needed for effective disaster management.

The recommended protocol for standardizing disaster preparedness for organizations serving the homeless begins with the framework recommended by the literature. This includes developing a full disaster preparedness plan (Sahebjamnia et al., 2015). The disaster preparedness plan should direct the organization's behaviors through the disaster management cycle of mitigation, preparedness, response, and recovery (Haddow et al., 2013; Reddick, 2011). Using the findings from the current study, a sample outline of a possible disaster preparedness plan for organizations serving the homeless is found in Appendix G. It incorporates the best practices identified in Dataset A, as well as the current practices identified in Dataset B.

The mitigation section of the disaster preparedness plan will include information on what resources and funding sources are available to help secure homeless shelters, as well as information for technological support for preparing for a disaster the organization can use (Patton & Johnston, 2017). Mitigation efforts should also include a fully developed contingency plan (Sahebjamnia et al., 2015). The contingency plan will focus on the creation of redundancy of key systems, such as communication, data access, and power (Stambler & Barbera, 2015).

The preparedness component of the disaster preparedness plan will incorporate the best practices mined from Dataset A. For example, it should include a comprehensive description of the homeless population being served. A good definition will explain the demographic traits of the homeless in the community, where they congregate, and what their special needs are. It is also important to include a chart of roles and responsibilities of key players. This included who was responsible for evacuations, the coordination of transportation, disseminating information to the homeless, and managing the medical and psychological care for this population during the disaster (U.S. Department of Labor, 2014). The next part of the standardized disaster preparedness plan will be protocols for mitigation, preparedness, response, and recovery. These action plans will provide the organization with directions on how to handle each stage of the disaster management cycle. The final component of a well-designed disaster preparedness program for organizations serving the homeless was a training module. This module identified who needed training, what the training would entail, and how the training was to be administered (DHS, 2017). By utilizing this as the standard for minimum disaster preparedness, the organizations serving the homeless will be better able to meet their goals and objectives, as well as be better able to recover quickly from a disaster.

The response section of the disaster preparedness plan will focus on instructions and resources related to activating and using the plan to respond to an emergency or disaster (Haddow et al., 2013). This section should include contact lists, hierarchies for the response, laws and policies that authorize the organization's members to act, and special directions for the staff to follow (Luditka et al., 2008). For example, the response section needs to include evacuation plans, sheltering-in-place plans, instructions on how to turn on the backup power, and instructions on how to access the redundant systems developed during mitigation.

The final section of the disaster preparedness plan will address the recovery process. The recovery process is the rebuilding and restoral phase of the emergency and disaster management cycle (Haddow et al., 2013). This section needs to include instructions on who to contact to have the homeless shelter assessed for safety and habitability, who to contact about disaster relief funds, who can take over serving the homeless until the homeless shelter is safe to use again, and what other processes need to take place before the shelter can reopen.

Require accountability. The second recommendation for practice is to require accountability for disaster preparedness among organizations serving the homeless. One of the common trends in the data collected was that little effort went into planning for the homeless. In most community-level disaster preparedness plans reviewed, the homeless were only mentioned as a vulnerable population. In other cases, the only planning done was to assign roles and responsibilities for managing the disaster response for the homeless to a third-party organization, often homeless shelters. While it can be argued that homeless shelters engage in disaster preparedness, neither the data collected nor the information in the literature review showed that this was happening (Every & Thompson, 2014; Haddow et al., 2013). Among the reason for this is that there is no mandate for homeless shelters or other organizations serving the homeless to engage in disaster preparedness (Gin et al., 2015; Haddow et al., 2013; Walters & Gaillard, 2014). To correct this problem, mandates need to be passed to hold organizations accountable for their preparedness activities.

Several options exist for promoting a professional urgency and necessity for completing appropriate disaster preparedness planning among service providers for the homeless. The first is to pass a law that dictates steps be taken to protect the safety of a vulnerable population. This type of law would be akin to OSHA standards, Life Safety laws, and Fire Codes that promote accountability of property and business owners to protect the safety and well-being of employees and occupants of buildings (FEMA, 2018). The second option is to pass licensure requirements (FEMA, 2018). This option would make disaster preparedness planning a requirement for getting and keeping a licensure to operate a homeless shelter, and/or to qualify for non-profit status. The final option is to utilize professional ethics and standards as the guiding force for organizations serving the homeless to engage in disaster preparedness activities. This would be similar to the standards held by hospitals and long-term care facilities that define disaster preparedness as a professional responsibility (FEMA, 2018).

Recommendations for Future Research

In completing the current study, several issues emerged that created the need for future research. The first issue was that the disaster preparedness documents publicly available for review were limited, and often only eluded to what was being done. Future research needs to engage directly with organizations serving the homeless to see exactly what disaster preparedness activities are being completed, by whom, and with what level of detail. This will require direct interactions with human research subjects, which will require additional ethical precautions to be taken. However, it will produce a more accurate understanding of disaster preparedness among organizations serving the homeless.

Another topic for future research that emerged during the completion of the current study is the need to explore the implementation of disaster preparedness plans for the homeless. A limitation of the current study was that it focused on preparedness, which is only one step in the total disaster management cycle. It would be advantageous to directly observe how target organizations put their disaster preparedness plans into action, how effective they are, and where problems seem to occur. This line of inquiry can identify needs to update the current disaster preparedness strategies used by organizations serving the homeless, as well as to justify mandates for the adoption of standardized preparedness strategies.

A similar line of inquiry can be conducted to observe how communities collaborate to meet the needs of the homeless during a disaster. This would require the researcher, or researcher group, to be in a city when a disaster occurred and to follow the various organizations as they implement their plans. This study frame could be expanded by observing the entire disaster management cycle and how the targeted organization(s) completed each phase, or to see which phases were completed and omitted.

The final recommendation for future research is to implement an experimental design in which different disaster preparedness models are tested at various homeless shelters in the same city. This study would allow the researcher to determine if one model worked better than the others for homeless shelters who have limited expertise and resources available for preparedness activities. The findings from this study could then be used to design a best practice model for homeless shelters.

Conclusions

The current study worked to diagnose the disaster preparedness status of organization's serving the homeless during disasters in the United States.

The purpose of the study was to assess the gaps in disaster preparedness that existed for the homeless in the United States and to determine the vulnerabilities that the gaps created. The importance of this study came from the reality that little is known about what organizations are doing to prepare the serve the homeless during critical instances. Subsequently, false assumptions about who is doing what are preventing effective disaster preparedness and responses for the homeless from being developed. For example, local governments believe homeless shelters are planning for the homeless, and homeless shelters believe local governments are responsible for the preparedness activities. When assessed, neither was engaging consistently or completely in disaster preparedness for the homeless. The lesson learned from the data analyses was that no one is taking responsibility for the disaster preparedness needs of the homeless, and subsequently, this vulnerable population is being victimized by disaster crises as well as by the bureaucracy of emergency and disaster management. Changes are needed to prevent the dehumanization of the homeless during a disaster. The recommendations made are to create a standardized disaster preparedness strategy for organizations serving the homeless during a disaster, and to mandate and enforce roles and responsibilities. The findings from this study highlighted a significant gap in the disaster management system, which can be filled by implementing the recommendations made and by future scholarship inspired by the topic and discoveries of this study.

#

REFERENCES

Adams, L. M., Canclini, S. B., & Frable, P. J. (2015). "Skip the infection, get the injection": A case study in emergency preparedness education. *Nurse Education in Practice, 15*(1), 58-62. doi:http://dx.doi.org.ezproxy.snhu.edu/10.1016/j.nepr.2013.12.004

Adams, R. M., Prelip, M. L., Glik, D. C., Donatello, I., & Eisenman, D. P. (2017). Facilitating partnerships with community-and faith-based organizations for disaster preparedness and response: results of a national survey of public health departments. *Disaster Medicine and Public Health Preparedness*, 1-10. https://doi.org/10.1017/dmp.2017.36

Adelaine, S. A., Shoaf, K., & Harvey, C. (2016). An assessment of collaboration and disasters: A hospital perspective. *Prehospital and Disaster Medicine, 31*(2), 121-125. doi:http://dx.doi.org.ezproxy.snhu.edu/10.1017/S1049023X16000066

Afzali, A. A. M., & Shojaei, D. (2016). Investigation of crisis management structure of the selected countries with an emphasis on natural disasters using multi-case study method. *J. Pol. & L., 9*, 162. http://dx.doi.org/10.5539/jpl.v9n9p167

Agboola, F., Bernard, D., Savoia, E., & Biddinger, P. D. (2015). Development of an online toolkit for measuring performance in health emergency response exercises. *Prehospital and Disaster Medicine, 30*(5), 503-508. doi: http://dx.doi.org.ezproxy.snhu.edu/10.1017/S1049023X15005117

Aldunce, P., Beilin, R., Handmer, J., & Howden, M. (2014). Framing disaster resilience: The implications of the diverse conceptualisations of "bouncing back". *Disaster Prevention and Management, 23*(3), 252-270. Retrieved from https://www.emeraldinsight.com/doi/abs/10.1108/DPM-07-2013-0130

Aldunce, P., Beilin, R., Howden, M., & Handmer, J. (2015). Resilience for disaster risk management in a changing climate: Practitioners' frames and practices. *Global Environmental Change, 30,* 1-11. https://doi.org/10.1016/j.gloenvcha.2014.10.010

Amore, K., Baker, M., & Howden-Chapman, P. (2011). The ETHOS definition and classification of homelessness: an analysis. *European Journal of Homelessness, 5.* Retrieved from https://s3.amazonaws.com/academia.edu.documents/46422800/The_ETHOS_Definition_and_Classification_20160612-12328-awnk9a.pdf?AWSAccessKeyId=AKIAIWOWYYGZ2Y53UL3A&Expires=1527537886&Signature=mE4VD5Gk3xnuLoV7CbvdlfPDT%2BY%3D&response-content-disposition=inline%3B%20filename%3DThe_ETHOS_Definition_and_Classification.pdf

Annis, H., Jacoby, I., & DeMers, G. (2016). Disaster preparedness among active duty personnel, retirees, veterans, and dependents. *Prehospital and Disaster Medicine, 31*(2), 132-140. doi:http://dx.doi.org.ezproxy.snhu.edu/10.1017/S1049023X16000157

Arbon, P. (2014). Developing a model and tool to measure community disaster resilience. *Australian Journal of Emergency Management, The, 29*(4), 12.

Asjoda, S., Robinson, E. L., Gay, J., & Ramirez, M. (2016). Motivating rural older residents to prepare for disasters: Moving beyond personal benefits. *Ageing and Society, 36*(10), 2117-2140. doi:http://dx.doi.org.ezproxy.snhu.edu/10.1017/S0144686X15000914

ASPR. (2017). Disaster response for homeless individuals and families: A trauma-informed approach. Retrieved from https://www.phe.gov/Preparedness/planning/abc/Documents/homeless-trauma-informed.pdf

Balzacq, T. (2015). The 'Essence'of securitization: Theory, ideal type, and a sociological science of security. *International Relations, 29*(1), 103-113. Retrieved from http://journals.sagepub.com/doi/abs/10.1177/0047117814526606b?journalCode=ireb

Bemelmans-Videc, M. L., Rist, R. C., & Vedung, E. O. (Eds.). (2011). *Carrots, sticks, and sermons: Policy instruments and their evaluation* (Vol. 1). New Brunswick, NJ: Transaction Publishers.

Berke, P., Smith, G., & Lyles, W. (2012). Planning for resiliency: Evaluation of state hazard mitigation plans under the disaster mitigation act. *Natural Hazards Review, 13*(2), 139-149. Retrieved from https://ascelibrary.org/doi/abs/10.1061/(ASCE)NH.1527-6996.0000063

Berke, P., Cooper, J., Aminto, M., Grabich, S., & Horney, J. (2014). Adaptive planning for disaster recovery and resiliency: an evaluation of 87 local recovery plans in eight states. *Journal of the American Planning Association, 80*(4), 310-323. https://doi.org/10.1080/01944363.2014.976585

Bernard, H. R. (2017). *Research methods in anthropology: Qualitative and quantitative approaches.* New York, NY: Rowman & Littlefield.

Birnbaum, M. L., Daily, E. K., O'Rourke, A.,P., & Loretti, A. (2016). Research and evaluations of the health aspects of disasters, part IX: Risk-reduction framework. *Prehospital and Disaster Medicine, 31*(3), 309-325. doi:http://dx.doi.org.ezproxy.snhu.edu/10.1017/S1049023X16000352

Blanchard, G., & Dosa, D. (2009). A comparison of the nursing home evacuation experience between Hurricanes Katrina (2005) and Gustav (2008). *Journal of the American Medical Directors Association, 10*(9), 639-643. https://doi.org/10.1016/j.jamda.2009.06.010

Boin, A., Stern, E., & Sundelius, B. (2016). *The politics of crisis management: Public leadership under pressure.* Boston, MA: Cambridge University Press.

Booth, S. A. (2015). *Crisis management strategy: Competition and change in modern enterprises.* New York, NY: Routledge.

Boscarino, J. A. (2015). Community disasters, psychological trauma, and crisis intervention. *International Journal of Emergency Mental Health, 17*(1), 369. Retrieved from https://www.ncbi.nlm.nih.gov/pmc/articles/PMC4429300/

Brassett, J., & Vaughan-Williams, N. (2015). Security and the performative politics of resilience: Critical infrastructure protection and humanitarian emergency preparedness. *Security Dialogue, 46*(1), 32-50. DOI: 10.1177/0967010614555943

Breevaart, K., Bakker, A., Hetland, J., Demerouti, E., Olsen, O. K., & Espevik, R. (2014). Daily transactional and transformational leadership and daily employee engagement. *Journal of Occupational and Organizational Psychology, 87*(1), 138-157. https://doi.org/10.1111/joop.12041

Bristow, G., & Healy, A. (2014). Building resilient regions: Complex adaptive systems and the role of policy intervention. *Raumforschung und Raumordnung, 72*(2), 93-102. DOI: 10.1007/s13147-014-0280-0

Brown, L. M., Beutler, L. E., Patterson, J. H., Bongar, B., & Holleran, L. (2016). Psychotherapy with people exposed to mass casualty events: Theory and practice. *Comprehensive textbook of psychotherapy: Theory and practice.* New York, NY: Oxford University Press.

Brunkard, J., Namulanda, G., & Ratard, R. (2008). Hurricane Katrina deaths, Louisiana, 2005. *Disaster Medicine and Public Health Preparedness, 2*(04), 215-223. https://doi.org/10.1097/DMP.0b013e31818aaf55

Burby, R. J. (2006). Hurricane Katrina and the paradoxes of government disaster policy: Bringing about wise governmental decisions for hazardous areas. *The Annals of the American Academy of Political and Social Science, 604*(1), 171-191. DOI: 10.1177/0002716205284676

Burke, F.M. Jr., Lynznicki, J.M., & James, J.J. (2012). Cross-disciplinary competency and professionalization in disaster medicine and public health. *Handbook for pandemic and mass-casualty planning and response.* Amsterdam: IOS Press. Retrieved from https://www.researchgate.net/profile/Frederick_Burkle/publication/283583193_Cross-disciplinary_Competency_and_Professionalization_in_Disaster_Medicine_and_Public_Health/links/5683083f08aebccc4e0e1f9b/Cross-disciplinary-Competency-and-Professionalization-in-Disaster-Medicine-and-Public-Health.pdf

Burla L., Knierim B., Barth K. L., Duetz M., Abel T. (2008). From the text to coding: Intercoder reliability assessment in qualitative content analysis. *Nursing Research, 57*, 113-117. doi: 10.1097/01.NNR.0000313482.33917.7d

Business impact analysis. (2017). *Ready.gov.* Retrieved from https://www.ready.gov/business-impact-analysis

Carter, N., Bryant-Lukosius, D., DiCenso, A., Blythe, J., & Neville, A. J. (2014, September). The use of triangulation in qualitative research. *Oncology Nursing Forum, 41*(5), 545-547. DOI: 10.1188/14.ONF.545-547

Cavallo, A., & Ireland, V. (2014). Preparing for complex interdependent risks: a system of systems approach to building disaster resilience. *International Journal of Disaster Risk Reduction, 9*, 181-193. https://doi.org/10.1016/j.ijdrr.2014.05.001

Chandra, A., Williams, M., Plough, A., Stayton, A., Wells, K. B., Horta, M., & Tang, J. (2013). Getting actionable about community resilience: the Los Angeles county community disaster resilience project. *American Journal of Public Health, 103*(7), 1181-1189. DOI: 10.2105/AJPH.2013.301270

Chong, M. T., Yamaki, J., Harwood, M., d'Assalenaux, R., Rosenberg, E., Aruoma, O., & Bishayee, A. (2014). Assessing health conditions and medication use among the homeless community in Long Beach, California. *Journal of Research in Pharmacy Practice, 3*(2), 56. https://dx.doi.org/10.4103%2F2279-042X.137073

Claver, M. L., Wyte-Lake, T., & Dobalian, A. (2015). Disaster preparedness in home-based primary care: Policy and training. *Prehospital and Disaster Medicine, 30*(4), 337-343. doi:http://dx.doi.org.ezproxy.snhu.edu/10.1017/S1049023X15004847

Coe, A. B., Moczygemba, L. R., Harpe, S. E., & Gatewood, S. B. (2015). Homeless patients' use of urban emergency departments in the United States. *The Journal of Ambulatory Care Management, 38*(1), 48-58. doi: 10.1097/JAC.0000000000000034

Congress, U. S. (2002). Homeland Security Act of 2002. *Public Law, 107*.

Connelly, L. M. (2014). Ethical considerations in research studies. *Medsurg Nursing, 23*(1), 54. Retrieved from https://search.proquest.com/openview/e2133580f4c400b81aee49468419127f/1?pq-origsite=gscholar&cbl=30764

Cope, D. G. (2014). Methods and meanings: Credibility and trustworthiness of qualitative research. *Oncology Nursing Forum, 41*(1), 89-91. doi:10.1188/14.ONF.89-91

Cranmer, H.H., & Biddinger, P.D. (2014). Typhoon Haiyan and the professionalization of disaster response. *New England Journal of Medicine, 27*, 1185-187. http://dx.doi.org/10.1056/NEJMp1401820

Crawford, E. R., Rich, B. L., Buckman, B., & Bergeron, J. (2014). The antecedents and drivers of employee engagement. *Employee Engagement in Theory and Practice*, 57-81. Retrieved from https://www.taylorfrancis.com/books/e/9781135128647/chapters/10.4324%2F9780203076965-12

Cuthbertson, R., & Piotrowicz, W. (2011). Performance measurement systems in supply chains: A framework for contextual analysis. *International Journal of Productivity and Performance Management, 60*(6), 583-602. DOI: 10.1108/17410401111150760

Cutter, S. L. (2013). Building disaster resilience: steps toward sustainability. *Challenges in Sustainability, 1*(2), 72. Retrieved from http://citeseerx.ist.psu.edu/viewdoc/download?doi=10.1.1.448.7283&rep=rep1&type=pdf

Cutter, S. L. (2016). The landscape of disaster resilience indicators in the USA. *Natural hazards, 80*(2), 741-758. https://doi.org/10.1007/s11069-015-1993-2

Cutter, S. L., Ahearn, J. A., Amadei, B., Crawford, P., Eide, E. A., Galloway, G. E., ... & Scrimshaw, S. C. (2013). Disaster resilience: A national imperative. *Environment: Science and Policy for Sustainable Development, 55*(2), 25-29. https://doi.org/10.1080/00139157.2013.768076

Cutter, S. L., Burton, C. G., & Emrich, C. T. (2010). Disaster resilience indicators for benchmarking baseline conditions. *Journal of Homeland Security and Emergency Management, 7*(1). https://doi.org/10.2202/1547-7355.1732

DHS. (2017). Plan and prepare for disasters. Retrieved from https://www.dhs.gov/topic/plan-and-prepare-disasters

Disasters. (2018). *FEMA*. Retrieved from https://www.fema.gov/disasters

Djalali, A., Carenzo, L., Ragazzoni, L., Azzaretto, M., Petrino, R., Della Corte, F., & Ingrassia, P. L. (2014). Does hospital disaster preparedness predict response performance during a full-scale exercise? A pilot study. *Prehospital and Disaster Medicine, 29*(5), 441-447. https://doi.org/10.1017/S1049023X1400082X

Donahue, D. A., Cunnion, S. O., Balaban, C. D., & Sochats, K. (2012). All Needs Approach to Emergency Response. *Faculty and Researcher Publications Collection*.

Doran, K. M., Mccormack, R. P., Johns, E. L., Carr, B. G., Smith, S. W., Goldfrank, L. R., & Lee, D. C. (2016). Emergency department visits for homelessness or inadequate housing in new york city before and after hurricane sandy. *Journal of Urban Health, 93*(2), 331-344. doi:http://dx.doi.org.ezproxy.snhu.edu/10.1007/s11524-016-0035-z

Dries, D., Reed, M. J., Kissoon, N., Christian, M. D., Dichter, J. R., Devereaux, A. V., ... & Balk, R. (2014). Special populations: care of the critically ill and injured during pandemics and disasters: CHEST consensus statement. *CHEST Journal, 146*(4_suppl), e75S-e86S. https://doi.org/10.1378/chest.14-0737

Edgington S. (2009). *Disaster planning for people experiencing homelessness.* Nashville, TN: National Health Care for the Homeless Council, Inc. Retrieved from http://citeseerx.ist.psu.edu/viewdoc/download?doi=10.1.1.183.7242&rep=rep1&type=pdf

Ehrke, F., Berthold, A., & Steffens, M. C. (2014). How diversity training can change attitudes: Increasing perceived complexity of superordinate groups to improve intergroup relations. *Journal of Experimental Social Psychology, 53*, 193-206. https://doi.org/10.1016/j.jesp.2014.03.013

Eidsvik, J., Mukerji, T., & Bhattacharjya, D. (2015). *Value of information in the earth sciences: Integrating spatial modeling and decision analysis.* Cambridge, U.K.: Cambridge University Press.

Eisenman, D., Chandra, A., Fogleman, S., Magana, A., Hendricks, A., Wells, K., ... & Plough, A. (2014). The Los Angeles County Community Disaster Resilience Project—A community-level, public health initiative to build community disaster resilience. *International Journal of Environmental Research and Public Health, 11*(8), 8475-8490. http://dx.doi.org/10.3390/ijerph110808475

Elachola, H., Al-Tawfiq, J. A., Turkestani, A., & Memish, Z. A. (2016). Public Health Emergency Operations Center-A critical component of mass gatherings management infrastructure. *The Journal of Infection in Developing Countries, 10*(08), 785-790. https://doi.org/10.3855/jidc.8332

Elo, S., Kääriäinen, M., Kanste, O., Pölkki, T., Utriainen, K., & Kyngäs, H. (2014). Qualitative content analysis: A focus on trustworthiness. *Sage Open, 4*(1), 2158244014522633. DOI: 10.1177/2158244014522633

Elo S., & Kyngäs H. (2008). The qualitative content analysis process. *Journal of Advanced Nursing, 62*, 107-115. https://doi.org/10.1111/j.1365-2648.2007.04569.x

Eshghi, K., & Larson, R. C. (2008). Disasters: lessons from the past 105 years. *Disaster Prevention and Management: An International Journal, 17*(1), 62-82. DOI: 10.1108/09653560810855883

Every, D. (2016). Disaster risk education, community connections and emergency communication with people who are homeless. Report for the Victoria State Emergency Service. *Accessed*, 22.

Every, D., & Thompson, K. (2014). Disaster resilience: Can the homeless afford it? *Australian The Journal of Emergency Management, 29*(3), 52. Retrieved from https://search.informit.com.au/documentSummary;dn=657064282083772;res=IELAPA

Fakhruddin, S. H. M., & Chivakidakarn, Y. (2014). A case study for early warning and disaster management in Thailand. *International Journal of Disaster Risk Reduction*, *9*, 159-180.
https://doi.org/10.1016/j.ijdrr.2014.04.008

Fekete, A., Hufschmidt, G., & Kruse, S. (2014). Benefits and challenges of resilience and vulnerability for disaster risk management. *International Journal of Disaster Risk Science*, *5*(1), 3-20. https://doi.org/10.1007/s13753-014-0008-3

FEMA. (2014). Emergency response plan. Retrieved from https://www.fema.gov/media-library-data/1388775706419-f977cdebbefcd545dfc7808c3e9385fc/Business_EmergencyResponsePlans_10pg_2014.pdf

FEMA. (2017). National preparedness. Retrieved from https://www.fema.gov/national-preparedness

FEMA. (2018). Laws & authorities. Retrieved from https://www.ready.gov/laws-authorities

Fletcher, S., Cox, R. S., Scannell, L., Heykoop, C., Tobin-Gurley, J., & Peek, L. (2016). Youth creating disaster recovery and resilience: A multi-site arts-based youth engagement research project. *Children, Youth and Environments*, *26*(1), 148-163. Retrieved from https://www.jstor.org/stable/10.7721/chilyoutenvi.26.1.0148

Fogel, S. J. (2017). Reducing vulnerability for those who are homeless during natural disasters. *Journal of Poverty*, *21*(3), 208-226.
https://doi.org/10.1080/10875549.2016.1141384

Fridman, A., Alkozei, A., Smith, R., Challener, S., & Killgore, W. D. (2017). 575. Resiliency is Associated with Reduced Activation within the Retrosplenial Cortex and Secondary Motor Area for Individuals with PTSD During Anticipation of a Negative Event. *Biological Psychiatry, 81*(10), S232-S233. https://doi.org/10.1016/j.biopsych.2017.02.445

Fuehrlein, B. S., Cowell, A. J., Pollio, D. E., Cupps, L. Y., Balfour, M. E., & North, C. S. (2014). Deriving costs of service use among an urban homeless population. *Journal of Substance Abuse Treatment, 46*(4), 491-497. https://doi.org/10.1016/j.jsat.2013.12.002

Fusch, P. I., & Ness, L. R. (2015). Are we there yet? Data saturation in qualitative research. *The Qualitative Report, 20*(9), 1408. Retrieved from https://nsuworks.nova.edu/tqr/vol20/iss9/3

Fussell, E. (2015). The long-term recovery of New Orleans' population after Hurricane Katrina. *American Behavioral Scientist, 59*(10), 1231-1245. DOI: 10.1177/0002764215591181

Gallardo, A. R., Djalali, A., Foletti, M., Ragazzoni, L., Della Corte, F., Lupescu, O., ... & Fisher, P. (2015). Core competencies in disaster management and humanitarian assistance: a systematic review. *Disaster Medicine and Public Health Preparedness, 9*(4), 430-439. https://doi.org/10.1017/dmp.2015.24

Gamboa-Maldonado, T., Marshak, H. H., Sinclair, R., Montgomery, S., & Dyjack, D. T. (2012). Building capacity for community disaster preparedness: a call for collaboration between public environmental health and emergency preparedness and response programs. *Journal of Environmental Health, 75*(2), 24. Retrieved from https://www.ncbi.nlm.nih.gov/pmc/articles/PMC4651206/

Gandy, S., Kern, K., Norton, J., & Toth, A. (2014). Emergency disaster preparedness and response. *OLA Quarterly*, *14*(4), 1. Retrieved from https://commons.pacificu.edu/olaq/vol14/iss4/2/

Ghilani, C. D. (2017). *Adjustment computations: Spatial data analysis.* Hoboken, NJ: John Wiley & Sons.

Gin, J. L., Eisner, R. K., Der-Martirosian, C., Kranke, D., & Dobalian, A. (2017). Preparedness is a marathon, not a sprint: A tiered maturity model for assessing preparedness in homeless residential organizations in Los Angeles. *Natural Hazards Review*, *19*(1), 04017027. DOI: 10.1061/%28ASCE%29NH.1527-6996.0000276

Gin, J. L., Kranke, D., Saia, R., & Dobalian, A. (2015). Disaster preparedness in homeless residential organizations in Los Angeles County: Identifying needs, assessing gaps. *Natural Hazards Review*, *17*(1), 04015022. DOI: 10.1061/(ASCE)NH.1527-6996.0000208

Gowing, J., Walker, K., Elmer, S., & Cummings, E. (2017). What are the most effective methods of disaster preparation for health professionals and support staff? Perspectives from staff at St Vincent's Private Hospital, Sydney-phase 1 of a multi-site study. *Prehospital and Disaster Medicine*, *32*(S1), S74-S74. https://doi.org/10.1017/S1049023X17001972

Gregory, P. A. (2015). Reassessing the effectiveness of all-hazards planning in emergency management. *Inquiries Journal*, *7*(06). Retrieved from http://www.inquiriesjournal.com/articles/1050/2/reassessing-the-effectiveness-of-all-hazards-planning-in-emergency-management

Haddow, G., Bullock, J., & Coppola, D. P. (2013). *Introduction to emergency management.* New York, NY: Butterworth-Heinemann.

Hallett, R. E., & Crutchfield, R. (2017). *Homelessness and Housing Insecurity in Higher Education: A Trauma-Informed Approach to Research, Policy, and Practice: ASHE Higher Education Report.* Hoboken, NJ: John Wiley & Sons.

Hamann, C. J., Mello, E., Wu, H., Yang, J., Waldron, D., & Ramirez, M. (2016). Disaster preparedness in rural families of children with special health care needs. *Disaster Medicine and Public Health Preparedness, 10*(2), 225-232. https://doi.org/10.1017/dmp.2015.159

Hambrick, E. P., Rubens, S. L., Vernberg, E. M., Jacobs, A. K., & Kanine, R. M. (2014). Towards successful dissemination of psychological first aid: A study of provider training preferences. *The Journal of Behavioral Health Services & Research, 41*(2), 203-215. https://doi.org/10.1007/s11414-013-9362-y

Hamer, M. J. M., Reed, P. L., Greulich, J. D., Kelen, G. D., Bradstreet, N. A., & Beadling, C. W. (2017). The West Africa disaster preparedness initiative: Strengthening national capacities for all-hazards disaster preparedness. *Disaster Medicine and Public Health Preparedness, 11*(4), 431-438. https://doi.org/10.1017/dmp.2016.155

Harriman, S., & Patel, J. (2014). The ethics and editorial challenges of internet-based research. *BMC Medicine, 12*(1), 124. https://doi.org/10.1186/s12916-014-0124-3

Heagele, T. N. (2016). Lack of evidence supporting the effectiveness of disaster supply kits. *American Journal of Public Health, 106*(6), 979-982. doi:http://dx.doi.org.ezproxy.snhu.edu/10.2105/AJPH.2016.303148

Hoskins, B. L., & Lacey, K. D. (2016). *Mass evacuation and sheltering.* Quincy, MA: Fire Protection Research Foundation.

HUD Exchange. (2017). Disaster planning for homeless populations. Retrieved from https://www.hudexchange.info/news/disaster-planning-for-homeless-populations/

Ignatow, G. (2016). Theoretical foundations for digital text analysis. *Journal for the Theory of Social Behaviour, 46*(1), 104-120. https://doi.org/10.1111/jtsb.12086

Inglesby, T. V. (2011). Progress in disaster planning and preparedness since 2001. *JAMA, 306*(12), 1372-1373. doi:10.1001/jama.2011.1359

Jaeger, P. T., Langa, L. A., McClure, C. R., & Bertot, J. C. (2007). The 2004 and 2005 Gulf Coast hurricanes: Evolving roles and lessons learned for public libraries in disaster preparedness and community services. *Public Library Quarterly, 25*(3-4), 199-214. DOI: 10.1300/J118v25n03_17

Jahre, M., Pazirandeh, A., & Van Wassenhove, L. (2016). Defining logistics preparedness: A framework and research agenda. *Journal of Humanitarian Logistics and Supply Chain Management, 6*(3), 372-398. https://doi.org/10.1108/JHLSCM-04-2016-0012

Johnson, V. A. (2014). *Evaluating disaster education programs for children: A thesis presented for the degree of Doctor of Philosophy in Emergency Management at Massey University, Wellington, New Zealand* (Doctoral dissertation, Massey University). Retrieved from http://hdl.handle.net/10179/5967

Kar, N. (2016). Care of older persons during and after disasters: meeting the challenge. *Journal of Geriatric Care and Research 2016, 3*(1): 7, 12. Retrieved from https://ssrn.com/abstract=2891469

Knuth, D., Kehl, D., Hulse, L., & Schmidt, S. (2014). Risk perception, experience, and objective risk: A cross-national study with European emergency survivors. *Risk Analysis, 34*(7), 1286-1298. https://doi.org/10.1111/risa.12157

Kuhlicke, C. (2013). Resilience: a capacity and a myth: findings from an in-depth case study in disaster management research. *Natural Hazards, 67*(1), 61-76. https://doi.org/10.1007/s11069-010-9646-y

Laditka, S. B., Laditka, J. N., Xirasagar, S., Cornman, C. B., Davis, C. B., & Richter, J. V. (2008). Providing shelter to nursing home evacuees in disasters: lessons from Hurricane Katrina. *American Journal of Public Health, 98*(7), 1288. DOI: 10.2105/AJPH.2006.107748

Lane, S. J., & McGrady, E. (2016). Nursing home self-assessment of implementation of emergency preparedness standards. *Prehospital and Disaster Medicine, 31*(4), 422-431. doi:http://dx.doi.org.ezproxy.snhu.edu/10.1017/S1049023X16000492

Le, A. B., Witter, L., Herstein, J. J., Jelden, K. C., Beam, E. L., Gibbs, S. G., & Lowe, J. J. (2017). A gap analysis of the United States death care sector to determine training and education needs pertaining to highly infectious disease mitigation and management. *Journal of Occupational and Environmental Hygiene, 14*(9), 674-680. https://doi.org/10.1080/15459624.2017.1319570

Lee, S., & Fleming, R. T. (2015). Collaborative disaster management in local governments: perception, performance, and challenges. *International Journal of Emergency Management, 11*(4), 343-355. https://doi.org/10.1504/IJEM.2015.074048

Llewellyn, G., Dominey-Howes, D., Villeneuve, M., & Lewis-Gargett, A. (2016). Disability and disaster risk reduction/emergency preparedness. The University of Sydney's Centre for Disability Research and Policy (CDRP) and Asia Pacific Natural Hazards and Disaster Risk Research Group. Retrieved from http://sydney.edu.au/health-sciences/cdrp/projects/DIDP-Scope-nov16.docx

Lowe, S. R., Sampson, L., Gruebner, O., & Galea, S. (2015). Psychological resilience after Hurricane Sandy: the influence of individual-and community-level factors on mental health after a large-scale natural disaster. *PloS One*, *10*(5), e0125761. https://doi.org/10.1371/journal.pone.0125761

Malilay, J., Heumann, M., Perrotta, D., Wolkin, A. F., Schnall, A. H., Podgornik, M. N., ... & Greenspan, J. R. (2014). The role of applied epidemiology methods in the disaster management cycle. *American Journal of Public Health*, *104*(11), 2092-2102. DOI: 10.2105/AJPH.2014.302010

McAneney, J., McAneney, D., Musulin, R., Walker, G., & Crompton, R. (2016). Government-sponsored natural disaster insurance pools: A view from down-under. *International Journal of Disaster Risk Reduction*, *15*, 1-9. https://doi.org/10.1016/j.ijdrr.2015.11.004

McCabe, O. L., Everly Jr, G. S., Brown, L. M., Wendelboe, A. M., Abd Hamid, N. H., Tallchief, V. L., & Links, J. M. (2014). Psychological first aid: a consensus-derived, empirically supported, competency-based training model. *American Journal of Public Health*, *104*(4), 621-628. DOI: 10.2105/AJPH.2013.301219

McQuiggan, M. (2016). Our kids: The American dream in crisis (Robert D. Putnam). *Policy Perspectives*, *23*, 137-142.

Mechler, R. (2016). Reviewing estimates of the economic efficiency of disaster risk management: Opportunities and limitations of using risk-based cost–benefit analysis. *Natural Hazards, 81*(3), 2121-2147. Retrieved from https://link.springer.com/article/10.1007/s11069-016-2170-y

Mechler, R., Mochizuki, J., & Hochrainer, S. (2016). Disaster risk management and fiscal policy: narratives, tools, and evidence associated with assessing fiscal risk and building resilience. *SSN*. Retrieved from http://repo.floodalliance.net/jspui/handle/44111/2720

Medina, A. (2016). Promoting a culture of disaster preparedness. *Journal of Business Continuity & Emergency Planning, 9*(3), 281-290. Retrieved from https://www.ingentaconnect.com/content/hsp/jbcep/2016/00000009/00000003/art00009

Meyer, L., Vatcheva, K., Castellanos, S., & Reininger, B. (2015). Barriers to disaster preparedness among medical special needs populations. *Frontiers in Public Health, 3*. https://doi.org/10.3389/fpubh.2015.00205

Miceli, R., Sotgiu, I., & Settanni, M. (2008). Disaster preparedness and perception of flood risk: A study in an alpine valley in Italy. *Journal of Environmental Psychology, 28*(2), 164-173. https://doi.org/10.1016/j.jenvp.2007.10.006

Mole, K., North, D., & Baldock, R. (2017). Which SMEs seek external support? Business characteristics, management behaviour and external influences in a contingency approach. *Environment and Planning C: Politics and Space, 35*(3), 476-499. DOI: 10.1177/0263774x16665362

Moynihan, D. P. (2012). A theory of culture-switching: Leadership and red-tape during hurricane Katrina. *Public Administration, 90*(4), 851-868. https://doi.org/10.1111/j.1467-9299.2011.02017.x

Murphy, B., Pearce, L., Chretien, A., & McLean-Purdon, E. (2017). Mutual aid and service agreements: Wise practices for First Nations communities. *Laurier.* Retrieved from https://www.crhnet.ca/sites/default/files/library/Mutual%20Aid%20Guide%20ENGLISH.pdf

Nakanishi, Y. J., & Auza, P. M. (2015). *Interactive training for all-hazards emergency planning, preparation, and response for maintenance and operations field personnel* (No. Project 20-05 (Topic 44-12)). New York, NY: Transportation Research Board.

Nejad, A. E., Niroomand, I., & Kuzgunkaya, O. (2014). Responsive contingency planning in supply risk management by considering congestion effects. *Omega, 48,* 19-35. https://doi.org/10.1016/j.omega.2014.03.002

Neuendorf, K. A. (2016). *The content analysis guidebook.* Thousand Oaks, CA: Sage.

Nicolay, M., Brown, L. M., Johns, R., & Ialynytchev, A. (2016). A study of heat related illness preparedness in homeless veterans. *International Journal of Disaster Risk Reduction, 18,* 72-74. https://doi.org/10.1016/j.ijdrr.2016.05.009

Nuttman-Shwartz, O. (2015). Shared resilience in a traumatic reality: A new concept for trauma workers exposed personally and professionally to collective disaster. *Trauma, Violence, & Abuse, 16*(4), 466-475. DOI: 10.1177/1524838014557287

Okal, E. A., Fritz, H. M., Raveloson, R., Joelson, G., Pancoskova, P., & Rambolamanana, G. (2005, December). Field survey of the 2004 Indonesian tsunami in Madagascar. *AGU Fall Meeting Abstracts* (Vol. 1, p. 0827). Retrieved from http://adsabs.harvard.edu/abs/2005AGUFM.U11A0827O

Paton, D. (2013). Disaster resilient communities: Developing and testing an all-hazards theory. *IDRiM Journal, 3*(1), 1-17. Retrieved from http://www.idrimjournal.com/index.php/idrim/article/view/50

Paton, D., & Johnston, D. (2017). *Disaster resilience: an integrated approach.* Charles C Thomas Publisher.

Persson, T. A., & Povitkina, M. (2017). "Gimme Shelter": The Role of Democracy and Institutional Quality in Disaster Preparedness. *Political Research Quarterly*, 1065912917716335. DOI: 10.1177/1065912917716335

Plough, A., Fielding, J. E., Chandra, A., Williams, M., Eisenman, D., Wells, K. B., ... & Magaña, A. (2013). Building community disaster resilience: perspectives from a large urban county department of public health. *American Journal of Public Health, 103*(7), 1190-1197. DOI: 10.2105/AJPH.2013.301268

Powell, J. H., Mustafee, N., Chen, A. S., & Hammond, M. (2016). System-focused risk identification and assessment for disaster preparedness: Dynamic threat analysis. *European Journal of Operational Research, 254*(2), 550-564. https://doi.org/10.1016/j.ejor.2016.04.037

Public Health Emergency. (2017). Disaster response for homeless individuals and families: A trauma-informed approach. Retrieved from https://www.phe.gov/Preparedness/planning/abc/Pages/homeless-trauma-informed.aspx

Public Law 106-390. (2000). Disaster mitigation act of 2000. Retrieved from http://www.fema.gov/media-library/assets/documents/4596

Public Law 107-296. (2002). Homeland security act of 2002. Retrieved from https://www.dhs.gov/xlibrary/assets/hr_5005_enr.pdf

Rafferty-Semon, P., Jarzembak, Jeremy, MA, BSN,B.S., R.N., & Shanholtzer, Jennifer,M.S.N., R.Nc. (2017). Simulating complex community disaster preparedness: Collaboration for point of distribution. *Online Journal of Issues in Nursing, 22*(1), 10-1E,2E,3E,4E,5E,6E,7E,8E,9E,10E. doi:http://dx.doi.org.ezproxy.snhu.edu/10.3912/OJIN.Vol22No01Man03

Rahm, D., & Reddick, C.G. (2011). U.S. city managers' perceptions of disaster risks: Consequences for urban emergencies management. *Journal of Contingencies and Crisis Management, 19*(3), 136-146. DOI: 10.1111/jccm.2011.19.issue-3

Raju, E., & Becker, P. (2013). Multi-organizational coordination for disaster recovery: The story of post-tsunami Tamil Nadu, India. *International Journal of Disaster Risk Reduction, 4*, 82-91. https://doi.org/10.1016/j.ijdrr.2013.02.004

Rayburn, R. L., Pals, H., & Wright, J. D. (2012). Death, drugs, and disaster: Mortality among New Orleans' homeless. *Care Management Journals, 13*(1), 8-18.

Rebmann, T., Elliott, M. B., Artman, D., VanNatta, M., & Wakefield, M. (2016). Impact of an Education Intervention on Missouri K-12 School Disaster and Biological Event Preparedness. *Journal of School Health, 86*(11), 794-802. https://doi.org/10.1111/josh.12435

Reddick, C. (2011). Information technology and emergency management: preparedness and planning in US States. *Disasters, 35*(1), 45-61. https://doi.org/10.1111/j.1467-7717.2010.01192.x

Reininger, B. M., Rahbar, M. H., Lee, M., Chen, Z., Alam, S. R., Pope, J., & Adams, B. (2013). Social capital and disaster preparedness among low income Mexican Americans in a disaster prone area. *Social Science & Medicine, 83,* 50-60. https://doi.org/10.1016/j.socscimed.2013.01.037

Reyes, D. D., & Lu, J. L. (2017). Gender dimensions and women's vulnerability in disaster situations: A case study of flood prone areas impacting women in Malabon City, Metro Manila. *Journal of International Women's Studies, 18*(4), 69-88. Retrieved from http://vc.bridgew.edu/jiws/vol18/iss4/6/

Rojas-Guyler, L., Inniss-Richter, Z. M., Lee, R., Bernard, A., & King, K. (2014). Factors predictive of knowledge and self-management behaviors among male military veterans with diabetes Residing in a homeless shelter for people recovering from addiction. *Health Educator, 46*(1), 49-56. Retrieved from https://eric.ed.gov/?id=EJ1046910

Sahebjamnia, N., Torabi, S. A., & Mansouri, S. A. (2015). Integrated business continuity and disaster recovery planning: Towards organizational resilience. *European Journal of Operational Research, 242*(1), 261-273. https://doi.org/10.1016/j.ejor.2014.09.055

Sandström, B. E., Eriksson, H., Norlander, L., Thorstensson, M., & Cassel, G. (2014). Training of public health personnel in handling CBRN emergencies: A table-top exercise card concept. *Environment International, 72,* 164-169. https://doi.org/10.1016/j.envint.2014.03.009

Sauro, J., & Lewis, J. R. (2016). *Quantifying the user experience: Practical statistics for user research.* Cambridge, MA: Morgan Kaufmann.

Schreier, M. (2014). Qualitative content analysis. *The SAGE handbook of qualitative data analysis.* Thousand Oaks, CA: SAGE Publishing.

Schuster, M. A., Stein, B. D., Jaycox, L. H., Collins, R. L., Marshall, G. N., Elliott, M. N., ... & Berry, S. H. (2001). A national survey of stress reactions after the September 11, 2001, terrorist attacks. *New England Journal of Medicine, 345*(20), 1507-1512. DOI: 10.1056/NEJM200111153452024

Scolobig, A., Prior, T., Schröter, D., Jörin, J., & Patt, A. (2015). Towards people-centered approaches for effective disaster risk management: Balancing rhetoric with reality. *International Journal of Disaster Risk Reduction, 12,* 202-212. https://doi.org/10.1016/j.ijdrr.2015.01.006

Settembrino, M. R. (2017). Exercising agency: How men experiencing homelessness employ human, social, and cultural capital to mitigate natural hazards risk. *Natural Hazards Review, 18*(4), 05017004. DOI: 10.1061/(ASCE)NH.1527-6996.0000256

Sittig, D. F., Gonzalez, D., & Singh, H. (2014). Contingency planning for electronic health record-based care continuity: a survey of recommended practices. *International Journal of Medical Informatics, 83*(11), 797-804. https://doi.org/10.1016/j.ijmedinf.2014.07.007

Skipper, J. B., Hall, D. J., Hazen, B. T., & Hanna, J. B. (2014). Achieving flexibility via contingency planning activities in the supply chain. *International Journal of Information Systems and Supply Chain Management (IJISSCM), 7*(2), 1-21.

Smith, N. (2007). Disastrous accumulation. *South Atlantic Quarterly, 106*(4), 769-787. https://doi.org/10.1215/00382876-2007-045

Soltani, A., Ardalan, A., Boloorani, A. D., Haghdoost, A., & Hosseinzadeh-Attar, M. J. (2015). Criteria for site selection of temporary shelters after earthquakes: A delphi panel. *PLoS Currents, 7.* DOI: https://dx.doi.org/10.1371%2Fcurrents.dis.07ae4415115b4b3d71f99ba8b304b807

Sommer, S. A., Howell, J. M., & Hadley, C. N. (2016). Keeping positive and building strength: The role of affect and team leadership in developing resilience during an organizational crisis. *Group & Organization Management, 41*(2), 172-202. DOI: 10.1177/1059601115578027

Song, A., Wenzel, S. L., Kim, J. Y., & Nam, B. (2017). Experience of domestic violence during childhood, intimate partner violence, and the deterrent effect of awareness of legal consequences. *Journal of Interpersonal Violence, 32*(3), 357-372. DOI: 10.1177/0886260515586359

Stambler, K. S., & Barbera, J. A. (2015). The evolution of shortcomings in Incident Command System: Revisions have allowed critical management functions to atrophy. *Journal of Emergency Management (Weston, Mass.), 13*(6), 509-518. https://doi.org/10.5055/jem.2015.0260

Steelman, T. A., Nowell, B., Bayoumi, D., & McCaffrey, S. (2014). Understanding information exchange during disaster response: methodological insights from infocentric analysis. *Administration & Society, 46*(6), 707-743. DOI: 10.1177/0095399712469198

Sundareswaran, M., Ghazzawi, A., & O'Sullivan, T. L. (2015). Upstream disaster management to support people experiencing homelessness. *PLoS Currents, 7*. https://dx.doi.org/10.1371%2Fcurrents.dis.95f6b767 89ce910bae08b6dc1f252c7d

Sylves, R. (2014). *Disaster policy and politics: Emergency management and homeland security*. Thousand Oaks, CA: CQ Press.

Taylor, K., Godin, M., Garnholz, D., Lin, A., & Cohen, R. (2017). Utilizing an interprofessional team to create a disaster preparedness report in the electronic health record. *Journal of Informatics Nursing, 2*(2), 6.

Thompson, K., Every, D., Rainbird, S., Cornell, V., Smith, B., & Trigg, J. (2014). No pet or their person left behind: Increasing the disaster resilience of vulnerable groups through animal attachment, activities and networks. *Animals, 4*(2), 214-240. Retrieved from http://www.mdpi.com/2076-2615/4/2/214

Tosh, P. K., Feldman, H., Christian, M. D., Devereaux, A. V., Kissoon, N., & Dichter, J. R. (2014). Business and continuity of operations: care of the critically ill and injured during pandemics and disasters: CHEST consensus statement. *Chest, 146*(4), e103S-e117S. https://doi.org/10.1378/chest.14-0739

Torabi, S. A., Soufi, H. R., & Sahebjamnia, N. (2014). A new framework for business impact analysis in business continuity management (with a case study). *Safety Science, 68*, 309-323. https://doi.org/10.1016/j.ssci.2014.04.017

Tong, A., & Dew, M. A. (2016). Qualitative research in transplantation: Ensuring relevance and rigor. *Transplantation, 100*(4), 710-712. doi: 10.1097/TP.0000000000001117

U.S. Census Bureau. (2016). Population counter. Retrieved from https://www.census.gov/programs-surveys/popest.html

U.S. Department of Health and Human Services. (2013). Disaster response for homeless individuals and families: A trauma-informed approach. Retrieved from http://www.phe.gov/Preparedness/planning/abc/Pages/homeless-trauma-informed.aspx

U.S. Department of Housing and Urban Development. (2014). The 2014 annual homeless assessment report (AHAR) to Congress. Retrieved from https://www.hudexchange.info/resources/documents/2014-AHAR-Part1.pdf

U.S. Department of Housing and Urban Development. (2016). The 2016 annual homeless assessment report (AHAR) to Congress. Retrieved from https://www.hudexchange.info/resources/documents/2016-AHAR-Part-1.pdf

U.S. Department of Labor. (2014). IT contingency plan. Retrieved from https://wdr.doleta.gov/directives/attach/UIPL/UIPL26-09a1.pdf

Vaismoradi, M., Turunen, H., & Bondas, T. (2013). Content analysis and thematic analysis: Implications for conducting a qualitative descriptive study. *Nursing & Health Sciences, 15*(3), 398-405. https://doi.org/10.1111/nhs.12048

van der Vegt, G. S., Essens, P., Wahlström, M., & George, G. (2015). Managing risk and resilience. *Academy of Management Journal, 58*(4), 971-980. https://doi.org/10.5465/amj.2015.4004

VanDevanter, Nancy,R.N., DrP.H., Raveis, V. H., PhD., Kovner, Christine T,R.N., PhD., McCollum, Meriel,B.S.N., R.N., & Keller, Ronald, PhD, MPA,R.N., N.E.-B.C. (2017). Challenges and resources for nurses participating in a hurricane sandy hospital evacuation. *Journal of Nursing Scholarship, 49*(6), 635-643. http://dx.doi.org.ezproxy.snhu.edu/10.1111/jnu.123 29

Veenema, T. G., Losinski, S. L. A., & Hilmi, L. M. (2016). Increasing emergency preparedness. *AJN The American Journal of Nursing, 116*(1), 49-53. doi: 10.1097/01.NAJ.0000476169.28424.0b

Vickery, J. (2015). Every day is a disaster. *Observer*, 10. Retrieved from https://hazards.colorado.edu/uploads/issue/e44587e 6cf1440ce8f49982707e16ee6fa2bd914.pdf#page=10

Vickery, J. (2017). Using an intersectional approach to advance understanding of homeless persons' vulnerability to disaster. *Environmental Sociology*, 1-12. https://doi.org/10.1080/23251042.2017.1408549

Von Lubitz, D. K., Beakley, J. E., & Patricelli, F. (2008). 'All hazards approach' to disaster management: the role of information and knowledge management, Boyd's OODA Loop, and network-centricity. *Disasters, 32*(4), 561-585. https://doi.org/10.1111/j.1467-7717.2008.01055.x

Walsh, L., Craddock, H., Gulley, K., Strauss-Riggs, K., & Schor, K. W. (2015). Building health care system capacity to respond to disasters: Successes and challenges of disaster preparedness health care coalitions. *Prehospital and Disaster Medicine, 30*(2), 112-122. http://dx.doi.org.ezproxy.snhu.edu/10.1017/S10490 23X14001459

Walters, V., & Gaillard, J. C. (2014). Disaster risk at the margins: Homelessness, vulnerability and hazards. *Habitat International, 44,* 211-219. https://doi.org/10.1016/j.habitatint.2014.06.006

Waugh, W. L., & Streib, G. (2006). Collaboration and leadership for effective emergency management. *Public Administration Review, 66*(s1), 131-140. https://doi.org/10.1111/j.1540-6210.2006.00673.x

Wyte-Lake, T., Claver, M., Dalton, S., & Dobalian, A. (2015). Disaster planning for home health patients and providers: A literature review of best practices. *Home Health Care Management & Practice, 27*(4), 247-255. DOI: 10.1177/1084822314567536

Yamakawa, Y., & Cardon, M. S. (2017). How prior investments of time, money, and employee hires influence time to exit a distressed venture, and the extent to which contingency planning helps. *Journal of Business Venturing, 32*(1), 1-17. https://doi.org/10.1016/j.jbusvent.2016.10.002

Zhang, Y., & Wildemuth, B. M. (2016). *Qualitative analysis of content. Applications of social research methods to questions in information and library science.* Denver, CO: Libraries Unlimited.

Zobel, C. W., & Khansa, L. (2014). Characterizing multi-event disaster resilience. *Computers & Operations Research, 42,* 83-94. https://doi.org/10.1016/j.cor.2011.09.024

Appendix A: Best Practices

Strategic Theme	Source 1	Source 2	Source 3	Source 4	Source N

Appendix B: Current Practices

Strategic Theme	Source 1	Source 2	Source 3	Source 4	Source N

Appendix C: Checklist of Best Practices

Best Practice	Current Practice Frequency	Prevalence Rate (%)

Appendix D: Analysis Level B

	Development Rating for Each Source				
Best Practice	Source 1	Source 2	Source 3	Source ...	Average Development Rating

Appendix E: BIA Questionnaire

Questionnaire removed for copyright purposes. It can be found on ready.gov

Appendix F: Standardized Disaster Preparedness Plan Outline for Organizations Serving the Homeless

I. Introduction

    A. Charter Statement for disaster preparedness plan

    B. Purpose Statement

    C. Goals and Objectives

    D. Situation and Assumptions

    E. Adoption Date

    F. Authorized Signatures

    G. Revision Chart

II. Mitigation

    A. Resources and Stockpiles

        1. List of resources needed to support clientele for 72 hours after a disaster strikes

        2. Contact information for resources that can be accessed in a disaster

B. Contingency Plan

   1. Critical functions

   2. Strategies for protecting critical functions

   3. Redundancy strategies

   4. Roles and responsibilities

C. Other Efforts to Prevent Disaster Problems

   1. Mutual aid agreements

   2. Strategic partnerships

III. Preparedness

   A. Description of the Homeless Population

      1. Demographics

      2. Where they congregate

      3. Communication plan for disseminating disaster information to the homeless

      4. Special needs

   B. Roles, Responsibilities, and Hierarchies

   C. Evacuation and Transportation Plans

D. Action Plans for Different Threats, i.e. fire, flood, hurricane, extreme weather

   F. Protocols for mitigation, preparedness, response, and recovery efforts.

   G. Training Program and Plan

IV. Response

   A. Contact Information of Community Emergency Services

   B. Contact Information for Other Important Stakeholders

   C. Activation Plan for the Disaster Preparedness Plan

   D. Checklists for What to Do

   E. Special Instructions as Appropriate

V. Recovery

   A. Contact Information for Disaster Recovery Aid and Assistance Sources

   B. Checklist for Restoring the Organization's Operations

C. Instructions and Information Relating to Who Can Temporarily Provide the Homeless with Shelter and Food while the Homeless Shelter Is Being Secured or Rebuilt.

D. Timeline for the Recovery Process

E. Deactivation Instructions for the Disaster Preparedness Plan for Returning to Normal Operating Conditions

VI. Appendices of Resources, Mutual Aide Agreements, and References

A. Mutual Aid Agreements

B. Insurance Information

C. Maps

D. Other